Essential
Madrid

by Paul Wade and Kathy Arnold

Freelance journalists Kathy Arnold and
Paul Wade have been regular visitors to Spain
for many years. They have written and edited
25 books, including AA publications such as
On The Road New England, and Thomas Cook
guides to London, Normandy and the Loire
Valley. They contribute to American magazines,
UK national newspapers, radio and
television programmes.

Above: *Plaza Mayor*

AA Publishing

Take your binoculars to appreciate the ceiling at El Escorial's library

Written by Paul Wade and Kathy Arnold
Original photography by Michelle Chaplow

Published and distributed in the United Kingdom by AA Publishing, a trading name of Automobile Association Developments Limited, whose registered office is Millstream, Maidenhead Road, Windsor, Berkshire SL4 5GD. Registered number 1878835.

A CIP catalogue record for this book is available from the British Library.

ISBN 0 7495 2299 2

A01088

Colour separation: Chroma Graphics (Overseas) Pte Ltd, Singapore
Printed and bound in Italy by Printer Trento srl

Find out more about AA Publishing and the wide range of services the AA provides by visiting our web site at www.theAA.com

Contents

About this Book

KEY TO SYMBOLS

✚	map reference to the maps found in the What to See section	⛴	ferry crossings and boat excursions
✉	address or location	ℹ	tourist information
☎	telephone number	♿	facilities for visitors with disabilities
🕐	opening times	✋	admission charge
🍴	restaurant or café on premises or near by	↔	other places of interest near by
Ⓜ	nearest underground train station	❓	other practical information
🚌	nearest bus/tram route	➤	indicates the page where you will find a fuller description
🚆	nearest overground train station	✈	travel by air

Essential *Madrid* is divided into five sections to cover the most important aspects of your visit to Madrid.

Viewing Madrid pages 5–14
An introduction to Madrid by the authors.
Madrid's Features
Essence of Madrid
The Shaping of Madrid
Peace and Quiet
Madrid's Famous

Top Ten pages 15–26
The authors' choice of the Top Ten places to see in Madrid, listed in alphabetical order, each with practical information.

What to See pages 27–90
The five main areas of Madrid, each with its own brief introduction and an alphabetical listing of the main attractions.
Practical information
Snippets of 'Did you know…' information
5 suggested walks
3 suggested drives
2 features

Where To... pages 91–116
Detailed listings of the best places to eat, stay, shop, take the children and be entertained.

Practical Matters pages 117–24
A highly visual section containing essential travel information.

Maps
All map references are to the individual maps found in the What to See section of this guide.
For example, El Prado has the reference ✚ 41E2 – indicating the page on which the map is located and the grid square in which the museum is to be found. A list of the maps that have been used in this travel guide can be found in the index.

Prices
Where appropriate, an indication of the cost of an establishment is given by € signs:
€€€ denotes higher prices, €€ denotes average prices, while € denotes lower charges.

Star Ratings
Most of the places described in this book have been given a separate rating:

😳😳😳	Do not miss
😳😳	Highly recommended
😳	Worth seeing

Viewing
Madrid

Above: *the centre of Spain is marked by Kilometre 0 in Puerta del Sol*

Right: *statue commemorating bullfighting legend Antonio Bienvenida outside Las Ventas bullring*

Paul Wade & Kathy Arnold's Madrid

Orienting Yourself
The heart of Madrid is compact. The *paseos* (boulevards), which run north–south, are the spine of the city. To the east is the vast Parque del Retiro (Retiro Park); to the west is the old quarter. Most of the attractions are within the square bordered by the Gran Vía (north side), the Palacio Real (west side) and the Rondas around the south.

Above: *bullfighting poster*
Right: *hand-painted directions to the Calle Mayor*
Below: *Plaza San Andrés*

Madrid was the capital of the world's first inter-continent empire. Between the 16th and 19th centuries, Spain rule South, Central and much of North America, with coloni as far afield as the Philippines. No wonder every chur seems more ornate than the last, and museums abour crammed with masterpieces. The palaces are gran ministries forbidding and houses enormous. When comes to sheer grandeur, Madrid stands shoulder shoulder with London, Paris and Rome.

The city has many faces. We enjoy exploring th medieval clutter of streets that scuttle away from the Pla Mayor, down to the rabbit warren of La Latina ar Lavapiés. Then there is the Habsburg quarter, west of th Puerta del Sol, and the high-class, trendy area of th *paseos* (boulevards) and Calle de Serrano. Walking arour the city is a pleasure, but you can also hop on the Metr the cheap, efficient and easy-to-use underground system linking every spot you will ever want to visit.

But most of all, this is a great place to have fun. *Madrileños* eat out constantly: you're never far from a coffee, a *caña* of beer or a glass of wine. Snacks abound, from sweet *churros* to salty *tapas*, served in bars walled with colourful tiles, and hung with faded photos of forgotten bullfighters. I summer, the *terrazas* (outdoor cafés) stay open until th early hours, causing traffic jams at three in the morning. A you need to get the best out of the city is stamina.

Madrid's Features

Geography

Madrid, the capital of Spain, is in the centre of the Iberian peninsula. Standing on a plateau some 650m above sea level, it is about 550–600km from both the Atlantic Ocean and the Mediterranean.

Climate

A Spanish saying describes Madrid as having nine months of winter and three months of hell. Certainly, winters are cold, with occasional snow, while summers are hot, with temperatures often over 35°C. Overall, the air is dry, with an annual average of 2,730 hours of sunshine. Spring and autumn are the best times of year to visit, with warm days and cool nights.

People and Economy

Over five million live in the province of Madrid, with three million in the city itself. Many come from other parts of Spain, as well as former Spanish colonies such as Argentina and Mexico.

Leisure Facilities

Madrid has at least 30 significant museums. Many are undergoing a much-needed upgrading to improve presentation and enjoyment by non-Spanish-speaking visitors. Few cities can rival the three jewels in Madrid's crown: the Museo del Prado (the Prado), the Museo Nacional Centro de Arte Reina Sofía and the Museo Thyssen-Bornemisza. In addition to cultural centres there are also amusement parks, swimming pools, a zoo and over 3,000 restaurants.

Province of Madrid
The metropolis is also the chief city of the province of Madrid, which encompasses 8,000sq km and includes cities such as Alcalá de Henares and Aranjuez. Just 52km to the north, the Sierra de Guadarrama provides skiing in the winter. Government and banking provide jobs in the city, and there are textile, food and metal-working industries in the surrounding area.

Above left: *contemplating Edward Hopper at Museo Thyssen-Bornemisza*
Above: *18th-century baroque entrance to the Museo Municipal*

Essence of Madrid

Madrid is one of the world's great capital cities with inhabitants who are intensely proud of their traditions. They order *cocido madrileño* (a classic Madrid stew), stroll in the Retiro Park on a Sunday morning and dance the *chotis* in the street during the festival of San Isidro. Most of all they love to stay up late, eating dinner at 11 and chatting in the *terrazas* (open-air cafés) until dawn. While the days are devoted to boring essentials such as working, Madrid really comes to life at night – if you can't beat 'em, join 'em.

People-watching on the Plaza Mayor

THE **10** ESSENTIALS

If you only have a short time to visit Madrid, here are ten essentials, which together create a portrait of the city:

• **Buy the special** *Bonoarte* **ticket and visit all three great art galleries**: the Prado (➤ 26), the Museo Nacional Centro de Arte Reina Sofía (➤ 19) and the Museo Thyssen-Bornemisza (➤ 22).

• **Tour the Palacio Real**, the monumental royal palace (➤ 23).

• **Drink a** *fino* **sherry** at La Venencia (➤ 97) or a vermouth with soda at Casa Alberto (➤ 96).

• **Order a** *cocido madrileño* (a classic Madrid stew), cooked in an earthenware pot by the fire at La Posada de la Villa (➤ 95).

• **Sip hot chocolate** and eat *churros* (like doughnuts) at the Chocolatería San Ginés (➤ 99).

• **Do what** *madrileños* **do on Sunday morning**: wander among the stamp and coin stalls on the Plaza Mayor (➤ 25); search for a bargain in the Rastro flea market (➤ 65); or stroll through the Retiro Park (➤ 24).

• **Go and watch a football** match at Real Madrid's Bernabéu Stadium (➤ 44), or at the Vicente Calderón stadium, home of rival Atlético Madrid.

• **Go shopping**, or window shopping, on Calle de Serrano (➤ 34) to see how the other half spends its money.

• **Take a siesta**; it's probably the only way you can stay up late.

• **Sit out at a** *terraza* (an open-air café), along the Paseo de la Castellana until two in the morning.

The Rastro market is a Sunday tradition

Souvenir-hunting on the Plaza Mayor

The Shaping of Madrid

Felipe II made Madrid his capital in 1561

Late 9th century
Muhammad I founds a Moorish village outpost called Magerit, 'the place of many springs'.

1083
Alfonso VI, King of Castile and Léon, captures Madrid, and gives the locals their nickname of *gatos* (cats) because of the numerous cats in the town.

1172
Death of Isidro Merlo y Quintana, aged 90. Later San Isidro Labrador, the labourer, is made patron saint of Madrid. His feast day is 15 May.

1309
Preparing to attack Granada, Fernando IV summons the parliament, the Cortes of Castile, to meet in Madrid for the first time.

1465
King Enrique IV awards Madrid the title of *muy noble y muy leal* (most noble and loyal). The city has some 20,000 inhabitants.

1477
Having united the kingdoms of Aragón and Castile by their marriage, Fernando and Isabel visit Madrid.

1544
Carlos I calls Madrid *imperial y coronada* (imperial and crowned).

1556
The first printing press is set up in Madrid.

1561
Felipe II moves his court to Madrid, the geographical centre of the country and now the capital of a vast empire.

1600
Felipe III is the first Spanish king born in Madrid.

1605
The first edition of Cervantes' classic story, *El Quijote* (*Don Quixote*), is published.

1613
The first town fire service is set up in Madrid.

1621
Under Felipe IV the arts flourish with names such as artist Diego de Velázquez and playwrights Lope de Vega, Calderón de la Barca and Tirso de Molina.

1701
Felipe V of Bourbon enters Madrid; the first ruler of a united Spain, the 17-year-old from France speaks no Spanish.

Court painter Diego de Velázquez was a superstar of Spain's Golden Age, despite his uncompromisingly realistic style

1819
The Museo del Prado opens to the public.

1879
The PSOE (Spanish Socialist Party) is founded at the Casa Labra bar in Madrid.

1900
The city has one million inhabitants.

1919
The Metro is inaugurated by Alfonso XIII.

1931
Republicans sweep the elections and King Alfonso XIII steps down.

1936–9
The Spanish Civil War takes place. Republican Madrid is besieged by Franco's Nationalist army for three years.

1946
United Nations sanctions against the Franco regime begin. Sanctions remain until 1955.

1960
The city has 2.2 million inhabitants.

1975
Franco dies and Juan Carlos I is Spain's first king since 1931. Modernisation of the city begins.

1738
The first stone is laid for the Palacio Real (Royal Palace). It is finished in 1764.

1759
Carlos III ascends the throne. Nicknamed the 'best Lord Mayor of Madrid', he commissions grand buildings that are now home to the Museo del Prado and the Museo Nacional Centro de Arte Reina Sofía.

1793
Diario de Madrid runs the first newspaper report of a bullfight.

1808
Napoleon's forces occupy Madrid. Napoleon's brother, Joseph Bonaparte, is named King José I of Spain. The annual 2 May holiday (*2 de mayo*) commemorates the Madrid uprising against the French, which also inspires two famous paintings by Goya (now in the Prado).

1814
Madrid is restored to Spanish rule under King Fernando VII.

1981
Spain's democracy is threatened by a military coup. Order is restored by Juan Carlos I. Picasso's *El Guernica* is moved to Madrid.

1986
On 1 January Spain joins the EEC (EU).

1992
Madrid is named as the European Capital of Culture. The Arab/Israeli peace conference is held in Madrid.

1998
Alcalá de Henares is declared a UNESCO World Heritage Site.

2002
The Euro replaces the *peseta* as the national currency of Spain.

Romantic view of Franco's capture of Madrid (1939)

Peace & Quiet

Two's company in leafy Retiro Park

Around every corner in Madrid there is a bench or a small square to rest weary feet or eat a sandwich. In addition the famous Parque del Retiro (► 24), is by no means the only green space in which to find peace and quiet.

Casa de Campo

To the west of the city, on the far side of the Río Manzanares, this vast park includes a restaurant, cafeterias, tennis courts, swimming pools, a lake, a zoo and the Parque de Atracciones (amusement park). With 1,820ha, these former hunting grounds are ideal for a

A lazy Retiro Park afternoon

picnic, kicking a ball about, or even tramping through the rough scrubland. During the Civil War, Franco's troops were based here, and some signs of the trenches are still visible. The most fun way to get there is by the Teleférico (► 71), but you can also go by Metro (Batán, Lago,) or drive there. Some parking places have become popular meeting spots for the gay community. It is best avoided at night.

Campo del Moro

Just below the Palacio Real, this park is more like a wood, even though the design is formal, with pleasant avenues and two attractive fountains – Las Conchas and Los Tritones. The royal carriage horses trot through for their daily exercise at noon.

Real Jardín Botánico

A step away from the Prado and the *paseos*, this relaxing spot has stunning displays of flowers and shrubs (► 70). As this is still a centre for scientific research, don't expect cafeterias or refreshments for sale. The entrance is on the Plaza de Murillo.

Jardines de Sabatini

Just north of the Palacio Real, these formal gardens were only laid out in the 1930s. Few visitors come here, so peace and quiet are guaranteed for most of the day. However, it is popular with mothers and small children after school.

Parque del Oeste

Set into the side of a hill, this rectangular park northwest of the Palacio Real has recently been renovated. The broad and elegant Paseo del Pintor Rosales runs along one side; the Ermita de San Antonio de la Florida (► 39) stands at the bottom of the slope. At the southern end is La Rosaleda, a rose garden which is at its best in May, and the Parque de la Montaña. Its temple was a gift from the Egyptian government. This is also the start of the Teleférico (► 71). The park is best avoided at night.

Plaza de Vázquez de Mella.

North of the Gran Vía, near the Telefónica (► 71), this newly refurbished square has benches, a fountain and a small playground where youngsters can burn off surplus energy.

Hotel Ritz

For a special treat, there is nothing quite like tea in the sheltered, flower-filled garden of one of the city's great hotels (► 102). It is a few steps north of the Prado (► 26).

Cooling off: Retiro fountain

There is always somewhere shady to rest your feet

Madrid's Famous

El Juli
Julián López López (1982–) is the most talked about *matador* in bullfighting. His youth, skill and rock-solid bravery in front of the biggest bulls bring new fans to the sport. However, El Juli's age has also renewed the controversy over whether bullfighting is a sport or a traditional ritual. Either way, seats to watch the virtuoso are always at a premium.

Carlos III

One king can be thanked for the grand buildings, parks and art galleries of Madrid: Carlos III (1716–88). He opened the Parque del Retiro (➤ 24) and its observatory and commissioned the building which now houses the Prado (➤ 26), the Real Jardín Botánico next door (➤ 70), and the elegant fountains along the *paseos* (➤ 59). The ordinary folk of the city also benefitted from a sewage and refuse system, as well as streets that were both paved and lit. No wonder he is remembered as the *Rey-Alcalde* (the King-Mayor) – perhaps the best mayor the city has ever had.

Goya

Every church and museum in Madrid worth its salt has a painting or fresco by Francisco José de Goya y Lucientes (1746–1828). A native of Aragón, his talent was soon recognised in Madrid. In 1792, a serious illness not only left him deaf, but also gave a new, hard edge to his work. By 1799, he was court artist to Carlos IV, but his portraits of the royal family were never flattering. As he grew older, he painted his most haunting works. His record of the French massacres in Madrid on 2 and 3 May in 1808, and the despairing 'Black Pictures' dominate the Prado (➤ 26).

Juan Carlos I, King of Spain since 1975

Juan Carlos I

When Alfonso XIII abdicated in 1931 in favour of the Republic, few believed that Spain would ever have a king again. However, when General Franco died in 1975, Spain reverted to a monarchy. Born in exile in Rome in 1938, Juan Carlos is tenth in the Bourbon line. In 1981 his forceful intervention to prevent a military coup endeared him to the Spanish people. Ever since, thanks to a down-to-earth lifestyle and devotion to duty, his popularity has never been in doubt. His wife, Sofía, is the daughter of King Paul of the Hellenes, and the couple have three grown-up children.

Top Ten

Above: *mirror image –
Museo Nacional Centro
de Arte Reina Sofía*
Right: *Felipe III's statue
in the Plaza Mayor*

1
Monasterio de las Descalzas Reales

Visit this 16th-century convent, still a closed order, not just to admire the notable art collection, but also to soak up the medieval atmosphere.

🕂 40C3

✉ Plaza de las Descalzas Reales 3

☎ 91 454 8800; www.patrimonionacional.es/descreal/descreal.htm

🕐 Tue–Sat 10:30–12:30, 4:30–5:45, Sun, public hols 11–1:45. Closed Fri PM, all day Mon

🍴 Plenty near by (€)

Ⓜ Callao, Sol, Opera

🚌 All routes to Puerta del Sol

ℹ Plaza Mayor 3
☎ 91 588 16 36

♿ None

✋ Cheap; free Wed to EU citizens

↔ Puerta del Sol (► 64)

❓ Visit by tour only, tours every 20 min, duration 45 min

Staircase in the Monasterio de las Descalzas Reales

Behind the austere brick and stone façade, some 25 brown-robed nuns go about their quiet daily life. Opening hours are limited, so expect to queue. Groups are ushered in 20 at a time for a basic tour of the convent, which was founded in 1559 by Juana de Austria, daughter of Carlos V. The convent houses the Descalzas Reales (Barefoot Royal Sisters), women who initially came from the royal family and nobility (modern nuns are generally of humbler origin). As a dowry, each brought fine religious works of art by European masters such as Titian, Brueghel the Elder, van Eyck and Zurbarán.

You begin the tour in the cloisters, then climb the massive staircase past walls painted by Ximénez Donoso and Claudio Coello. The broad stone balustrade is carved from a single piece of granite. At the top, Felipe IV and the rest of the royal family look down at you from their painted balcony. All around the upper cloister are 16 elaborate chapels, the most important of which is dedicated to Virgen de Guadelupe. Don't miss the doll's house-like altar in one corner, designed to teach children about the sacred vessels used during mass. In what was once the nuns' dormitory is the Salón de Tapices, hung with sumptuous Flemish tapestries based on Rubens' cartoons. Peek out of the window at the kitchen garden, which is still tended by the sisters, even though they are overlooked by office blocks.

2
Museo de América

This museum's outstanding collection focuses on the art and culture of the Americas from before the Spanish colonial period to the present day.

✚ 66A5

✉ Avenida de los Reyes Católicos 6

☎ 91 543 94 37; www.geocities.com/ museo-de-america

🕐 Tue–Sat 10–3; Sun, public hols 10–2:30

🍴 Café (€)

Ⓜ Moncloa

🚌 1, 12, 16, 44, 61, 82, 83, 132, 133

ℹ Plaza Mayor 3
☎ 91 588 16 36

♿ Good

✋ Cheap; free under-18, over-65; Sun

↔ Teleférico (► 71)

❓ Lectures Sat at 12 (except Aug)

Above: *aerial view*
Below: *Quimbaya gold statue (AD 200–1000)*

If this museum were located on the Paseo del Prado, it would be packed with visitors. Set in the university district northwest of the city centre, it remains a well-kept secret. The spacious building has two floors of permanent exhibits, divided into five sections: Instruments of Knowledge, the American Reality, Society, Religion and Communication. Maps explain the movements of native peoples through the Americas and the routes of the explorers; feathered head-dresses contrast with ceramic vessels shaped like sting rays or parrots.

Since the Spanish melted down much of the gold they found in the Americas, the surviving Quimbayas treasure is particularly important. Dating from 600 BC–AD 600, the 130 gold objects were discovered in two tombs in Colombia. Finely-crafted, they range from statuettes and bowls to necklaces and helmets. There is even a whistle and a trumpet.

Equally important are the codices, or manuscripts, which are keys to understanding pre-Colombian culture. One of only three surviving Mayan manuscripts is the *TroCortesiano Codex*, with symbols depicting the religious rituals of the Mayan calendar. Although the *Tudela Codex* also records religious ceremonies – this time of the late Aztec culture – it is post-conquest and dates from 1553. Written on paper and bound like a book, it is annotated in Spanish.

Paintings from the Spanish colonial period also serve as historical records, ranging from a large work showing the Archbishop and Viceroy Morcillo entering the city of Potosí (modern Bolivia) to a series of portraits of the multi-racial society of Mexico.

3
Museo Lázaro Galdiano

Banker Lázaro Galdiano left his home and collection to the city

✚ 67E5

✉ Calle de Serrano 122

☎ 91 561 60 84; www.flg.es

🕐 Tue–Sun 10–2. Closed Aug

🍴 Plenty near by (€)

Ⓜ Rubén Darío, Núñez del Balboa

🚌 9, 12, 16, 19, 27, 45, 51, 150

ℹ Calle del Duque de Medinaceli 2
☎ 91 429 49 51

♿ None

✋ Cheap; free under-18, over-65, Sat

↔ Museo Sorolla (➤ 20)

❓ Free guided tour noon daily. Extra opening during *Noches de Museo* (museum nights) Thu 7:30PM–11PM, end Jun to mid-Oct

The former home of financier José Lázaro Galdiano (1872–1947) is crammed with a profusion of rich treasures.

Although the quality and quantity of his private collection are extraordinary, the works have been compressed into 30 rooms, making it difficult to appreciate their individual glory. Major changes are in the pipeline, including a more selective approach to the arrangement and the installation of air-conditioning. Until then, buy a guide from the small shop before you begin.

The ground floor is devoted to religious art such as altar-pieces and richly worked crucifixes. In one corner is the *Gran Copa del Emperador Rodolfo II*, a mad German king's exotic 16th-century glass drinking cup. On the first floor are religious works, including two exquisite small paintings by Luis Cranach. On the floor above, in Room 20, Hieronymous Bosch's portrayal of St John the Baptist is as zany as anything by Salvador Dalí five centuries later. The roll call of the Old Masters includes cattle by Albert Cuyp, a ruffed nobleman by van Dyck and, in Room 23, a severe portrait by Velázquez. There is also an elongated figure of Christ with his mother by Jorge Manuel Theotocopuli, better known as El Greco (the Greek).

Room 25 is hung with British ladies painted by Gainsborough, Lawrence, Reynolds, Lely, Romney, and the American Gilbert Stuart. Room 27 is mainly Italian, with scenes of Venice by Tiepolo and Guardi. Finally, in Room 30, among the many works by Goya in the collection, are sketches for his 'Black Paintings' in the Museo del Prado (➤ 26).

4
Museo Nacional Centro de Arte Reina Sofía

One of the largest buildings in Europe houses Spain's national museum of modern art, including the world-famous painting, Guernica *by Picasso.*

Picasso's protest: Guernica was bombed in the Spanish Civil War

The two glass elevators that slide up and down the outside of what was an 18th-century hospital are typical of Spain's imaginative approach to building conversion. Two floors are devoted to the permanent collection of paintings and sculptures from the late 19th century to the present day; two more have temporary exhibitions.

Start up on the fourth floor. Rooms 34 and 35 are dominated by the gigantic canvases of Robert Motherwell (USA) and Antoni Tàpies (Spain). Pablo Palazuelo's geometric patterns make your eyes ache, while his fellow-*madrileño*, Eduardo Arroyo, prefers a big, bright palette. A star of the contemporary sculpture scene is Eduardo Chillida, whose massive metal works fill Rooms 42 and 43.

The biggest crowds are on the second floor. As you approach Rooms 6 and 7, you can hear the hum of conversation in the rooms dedicated to Picasso. The main focus is *Guernica* (1937), Picasso's powerful work condemning the unjustified bombing of the Basque town of Guernica during the Spanish Civil War. Picasso's will stated that the painting could only be brought to Spain when democracy was restored. In 1981, six years after Franco's death, *Guernica* was finally shown in Spain.

It is not the only politically inspired painting on display here. Rooms 10 and 11 are devoted to Dalí, whose *Enigma of Hitler* (1939) also reflects the uncertainty of those times. Nearby rooms feature works by Juan Miró, Juan Gris and the surrealist painters Max Ernst and René Magritte.

41E1

Calle Santa Isabel 52

91 467 50 62; www.museoreinasofia.mcu.es

Mon, Wed–Sat 10–9, Sun 10–2:30

Restaurant/café (€)

Atocha

All routes to Atocha

Good

Cheap; free under-18, over-65; Sat 2:30–9, Sun

Museo Nacional de Antropología (➤ 49), Museo Thyssen-Bornemisza (➤ 22), Museo del Prado (➤ 26)

The *Bonoarte* ticket is a reduced rate, combined ticket (➤ 22, panel)

5
Museo Sorolla

✚ 67D5

✉ Paseo del General Martínez Campos 37

☎ 91 310 15 84; www.mcu.es/nmuseos/sorolla

🕐 Tue–Sat 10–3, Sun, public hols 10–2

🍴 Plenty near by (€)

Ⓜ Iglesia, Rubén Darío

🚌 5, 16, 61

ℹ Calle del Duque de Medinaceli 2
☎ 91 429 49 51

♿ None

✋ Cheap; free Sun

↔ Museo Lázaro Galdiano (► 18)

The museum's garden is decorated with carefully sited statues

A well-furnished mansion, a fine art gallery and a painter's studio all in one, the home of Joaquín Sorolla (1863–1923) is a gem.

With its Moorish gardens and trickling fountains, the atmosphere at the Museo Sorolla is in total contrast to the formality and grandeur of Madrid's major museums. Born in Valencia, Sorolla worked in Paris and Rome before becoming the darling of European and American high society. Often labelled 'the Spanish Impressionist', Sorolla had no connection with that movement. Passionate about Spain and the Spanish, his treatment of sharp light and heavy shade was both individual and highly accomplished. While he lived in Madrid (1910–23), his large paintings, with their bold and lively brushwork of people in sun-dappled landscapes, were in great demand.

In the first room you see the romantic side of Sorolla. His studies for a series for the Hispanic Society of New York include a bagpiper and a *Don Quixote* look-alike from La Mancha, complete with donkey and windmills. Walk through the second room, with its jolly beach scenes, to Sorolla's studio. Here, the soaring walls are covered in canvases, including several of his wife, Clotilde.

His finest work is upstairs: note the portrait of Don Antonio García sitting in a rocking-chair overlooking the beach, and the large painting of four women taking a siesta. Don't miss *Madre* (1895), a simple scene of a tired mother and her new-born child. In galleries on the ground floor (enter from the garden) is Sorolla's fine collection of antique Spanish pottery, as well as some lively sketches of Central Park, New York.

Sorolla's antique pottery collection

Sorolla recorded Spanish folklore for a New York club

6

Museo Thyssen-Bornemisza

The Thyssen-Bornemisza collection's elegant 18th-century home

✚ 41E3

✉ Paseo del Prado 8

☎ 91 369 01 51; www.museothyssen.org

🕐 Tue–Sun 10–7. Closed New Year

🍴 Restaurant/café (€)

🚇 Banco de España

🚌 1, 2, 5, 9, 10, 14, 15, 20, 27, 34, 37, 45, 51, 52, 53, 74, 146, 150

ℹ️ Calle del Duque de Medinaceli 2
☎ 91 429 49 51

♿ Very good

✋ Moderate, under 12 free

↔️ Museo Nacional Centro de Arte Reina Sofía (➤ 19), Museo del Prado (➤ 26)

❓ Less crowded Wed–Fri lunchtime. Temporary exhibitions, café open until midnight Jul, Aug. The *Bonoarte* ticket is a reduced rate ticket for the Prado, Museo Thyssen-Bornemisza and Museo Nacional Centro de Arte Reina Sofía

The Thyssen-Bornemisza family built the world's finest art collection. It moved to Madrid in 1992, completing the city's golden triangle of museums.

Sympathetically remodelled, the spacious 19th-century Palacio de Villahermosa is the perfect setting for an art history lesson spanning seven centuries of European and American art. The lesson begins on the top floor, where the 13th– to 15th-century religious works positively glow, thanks to excellent lighting. Next come a succession of fascinating early Renaissance portraits. In Room 5, near Hans Holbein the Younger's classic portrait of Henry VIII of England, is Francesco Cossa's intriguing 15th-century *Portrait of a Man*. This is an experiment in *trompe l'oeil* and perspective as a hand holds out a ring for you to inspect. Room 20 has two Flemish masterpieces, lit as fiercely as a movie set: *Esau selling his Birthright* (1627) by Hendrik Terbrugghen and *Supper at Emmaus* (1633) by Matthias Stom.

On through the centuries, the tour continues past Titian and Caravaggio, Impressionists and Expressionists. Down on the ground floor are eight rooms of 20th-century works. In Room 41, works by Picasso and Braque exemplify the technical and aesthetic revolution of Cubism. Room 45 is lined with familiar 20th-century works: Picasso's *Harlequin with a mirror* (1923), Chagall's *Rooster*, a rich blue Miró titled *Catalan peasant with a Guitar*, plus others by Braque, Léger, Kandinsky, Ernst and Madrid's own Juan Gris. Room 47 focuses on star American names such as Edward Hopper, whose *Hotel Room* (1931) has a typically lonely and mysterious atmosphere. Expansion into an adjacent building coincided with the gallery's 10th anniversary in October 2002.

7
Palacio Real

With a grand parade ground, fabulous views over the city, imposing staircases and ornate rooms, this is everything that a royal palace should be.

The regal façade of the Palacio Real

All that is missing is the royal family, who prefer to live in the Zarzuela Palace on the outskirts of Madrid. Today, the grand 250-year-old Palacio Real is used solely for state occasions. To get the most out of your visit, join a 45-minute tour, then wander round at your leisure. As you climb the main staircase, imagine the red carpet treatment and guard of honour that greets new ambassadors and visiting heads of state. Each room seems more magnificent than the last. With its backdrop of 17th-century Flemish tapestries, the Sala de Columnas is often used for ceremonies, such as Spain's entry to the European Community (1986) and the Middle East peace accord (1992). Curiously, no one sits on the two thrones in the Throne Room because King Juan Carlos and Queen Sofía prefer to stand during audiences. Continue past great paintings by Goya and admire ornate clocks, then prepare yourself for Gasparini's Robing Room. This jewel box of a room, with a marble floor, decorated walls and encrusted ceiling, is now used for taking coffee after state banquets.

The banqueting hall has a grand ceiling fresco of Christopher Columbus offering the world to the *Reyes Católicos*, Fernando and Isabel. Outside the palace, the Real Armería (Royal Armoury) has undergone a facelift, installing the latest museum technology for its world-class collection. Temporary exhibitions are also held; most are free, with direct access from the street. Visitor-friendly improvements such as a cafeteria and toilets have also been installed. The Real Farmacia (Royal Pharmacy) is also well worth a visit.

- 40A3
- Calle Bailén s/n
- 91 454 88 00; www.patrimonionacional.es
- Summer: Mon–Sat 9–6, Sun, public hols 9–3. Winter: Mon–Sat 9:30–5, Sun, public hols 9–2. Closed on offical occasions
- Cafeteria (€)
- Opera
- 3, 25, 39, 148
- Plaza Mayor 3
  91 588 16 36
- Good
- Moderate
- Monasterio de la Encarnación (▶ 48)
- Multilingual guided tours. Changing of the Guard at 12, 1st Wed of month Feb–May, Sep–Dec. Telephone to confirm.

8
Parque del Retiro

The Palacio de Cristal (Crystal Palace) in Retiro Park

The 130ha park, with its mixture of formal gardens, tree-studded lawns and a large lake, acts as a set of lungs to refresh the city centre.

✚ 41F2

✉ Calle de Alfonso XII

🕐 Apr–Sep 6:30AM–midnight; Oct–Mar 6AM–10PM

🍴 Plenty (€)

Ⓜ Atocha, Ibiza, Retiro, Príncipe de Vergara

🚌 All routes to Retiro

ℹ Calle del Duque de Medinaceli 2
☎ 91 429 49 51

♿ Good

Free

↔ Casón del Buen Retiro (➤ 36), Museo Nacional de Artes Decorativas (➤ 50)

Felipe IV created this Buen Retiro (a pleasant place to retire or retreat) in the 17th century. This is where the court came to have fun, staying in the Buen Retiro Palace and watching bullfights, plays and fireworks in the gardens. A century later, Carlos III opened the royal park to the public – as long as they were dressed properly. By the mid-19th century, anyone could enjoy the park, whatever their garb.

Nowadays, a Sunday stroll is a must. *Madrileños* promenade along the Paseo del Estanque, while children play and watch noisy puppet shows. Take in a free concert of *zarzuela* music at the Templete de la Musica, have your portrait sketched or try your luck at the roulette wheels of the *chulapos*, colourful locals in waistcoats and caps. There are pathways for cyclists and rollerbladers, shady spots for picnicking and formal parterres with botanical name-plates to identify the species.

Important landmarks include the elaborate 1922 memorial and statue of Alfonso XII, *El Pacificador* (the Peacemaker), which overlooks the *estanque* (lake). Check whether there are any exhibitions in the two glass halls, the Palacio de Cristal and Palacio de Velázquez, both built in the 1880s, or the Casa de Vacas (House of Cows), which is on the site of an old dairy. La Rosaleda (Rose Garden) is at its best in May. Avoid the park after dark.

9
Plaza Mayor

Traffic-free and large enough to swallow a crowd of 50,000, one of the most handsome squares in Europe is dominated by a royal statue.

Felipe III's statue is a handy rendezvous spot on the Plaza Mayor

The bronze equestrian statue of Felipe III makes a popular meeting point. The reliefs around the four giant lampposts spell out the history of the plaza. In 1617, under Felipe III, the old square was replaced by this new arena, created to hold everything from bullfights to theatre, festivals to inquisitions. Its inauguration coincided with the beatification of San Isidro, Madrid's patron saint, in 1620, and the spacious balconies have been hired out to spectators ever since.

Throughout the year, tourists and locals alike watch the world go by from café tables that spill across the paving stones. During the annual San Isidro festivities in May, giant *cocidos* (stews) and *paellas* are served up, and in summer there are concerts and plays. The annual Christmas market, with its traditional sweets, cakes and toys, has been a feature since 1837. The Casa de la Panadería, the dominant building on the north side, dates from 1590, but the jolly murals were only added in 1992. The oldest shop on the square is Bustillo (No 4), where they have been selling cloth since 1790.

Sunday mornings are special. Since 1927, the arcades have been filled with dozens of tables for the popular stamp and coin collectors' market. In fact, anything that can be collected is displayed and offered for sale: postcards, cheese labels, pins and lottery tickets.

✚ 40C3

✉ Plaza Mayor

🍴 Botín (€), cafés near by (€)

Ⓜ Sol, La Latina

🚌 All routes to Sol

ℹ Plaza Mayor 3
☎ 91 588 16 36

♿ Very good

✋ Free

🔄 Casa de la Villa (➤ 36), Basilica de San Miguel (➤ 32), El Botín (➤ 33)

10
Museo del Prado

A Prado highlight: Las Hilanderas *(The Spinners) by Velázquez (c1657)*

🕂 41E2

✉ Paseo del Prado s/n

☎ 91 330 29 00

🕓 Tue–Sat 9–7, Sun, public hols 9–2. Closed Mon, 1 Jan, Good Friday, 1 May, 25 Dec

🍴 Restaurant/café (€)

🚇 Atocha, Banco de España

🚌 9, 10, 14, 19, 27, 34, 37, 45

ℹ Calle del Duque de Medinaceli 2
☎ 91 429 49 51

♿ Good

✋ Cheap; free under-18, over-65; Sat 2:30–7, Sun 9–2

↔ Museo Nacional Centro de Arte Reina Sofía (► 19), Museo Thyssen-Bornemisza (► 22)

❓ *Bonoarte* ticket: reduced rate for Prado, Museo Thyssen-Bornemisza and Museo Nacional Centro de Arte Reina Sofía. For the latest changes at the Prado, check their website: www.museo.nacional@prado.mcu.es

One of the world's great museums, Museo del Prado is reorganizing its vast collection by expanding into three nearby buildings.

The Edificio Villanueva, the main building on the Paseo del Prado, will continue to house masterpieces by Bosch, Goya, El Greco, Murillo, Rubens, Titian, Velázquez and Zurbarán. Near by, the Antiguo Salón de Reinos will have 18th-century art and the Casón del Buen Retiro 19th– to 20th-century works. In all, the Prado has over 8,000 paintings. To get the best out of a visit, focus on a favourite artist or era.

Not surprisingly, the range of Spanish art from the 11th to the 19th century is unparalleled, especially from the *Siglo de Oro*, the golden 17th century. Foremost was Velázquez (1599–1660), court painter to Felipe IV. His works, such as *Las Meninas* (The Maids of Honour) and *Las Hilanderas* (The Spinners) are turning points in the art of composition. A century later, Goya (1746–1828) was arguably, even more influential. His range was extraordinary, from his naked *Maja* (Courtesan) to the *Fusilamientos del 3 de mayo*. This patriotic, passionate painting commemorates the heroism of the *madrileñ* revolt against the French invaders in May 1808. Most disturbing of all are his 14 *Pinturas Negras* (Black Paintings) from the end of his life. *Saturn devouring one of his sons* and *Witches' Sabbath* make anything but comfortable viewing.

Don't miss *The Garden of Delights* by the Flemish master Hieronymus Bosch (1450–1516). Despite years of academic study, this allegorical triptych portraying human frailties has yet to be fully deciphered.

What
to See

Above: *hand-painted tiles still mark ancient streets*
Right: *the bull is a popular symbol all over Spain*

CALLE MAYOR

Hand-painted tiles at the Fontanilla restaurant

MADRID ENVIRONS

Loma del Corch

El Pardo

Río Manzanares

3

Segovia

A6

Aravaca

M500

Pozuelo de Alarcón

MONCLOA

M613

TETU

S:
Be

M40

M503

M30

Humera

Casa de Campo

CHAN
Pala
de I

La Cabana

2

Somosaguas

Parque de Atracciones

Pa
Rea
CEN

Monte Principe

Prado de Somosaguas

M602

Parque Zoológico

ARGAI

Los
Retamares

LATINA

NV E90

CARABANCHEL

M40

1

NV

M40

VILLA

Badajoz

N401

Alcorcón

Leganés

A

B

CALLE MAYOR

Burgos

El Encinar
de los Reyes

Paracuellos
de Jarama

Río Jarama

HORTALEZA

BARAJAS

Aeropuerto de
Madrid - Barajas

TIN

Campo de
las Naciones

CIUDAD
LINEAL
130

M40

A2

Guadalajara

E90

o de la
d

NCA

SAN BLAS

San Fernando
de Henares

Toros
ntal de
s

Coslada

MORATALAZ

VICALVARO

Las Canteras

LLECAS

726m
Almodóvar

M40

A

VILLA DE
VALLECAS

A3

E901

Valdecarros

0   2   4   6 km

Valencia

C

D

*Fresh fruit and vegetables
for sale in Calle de Serrano*

*View over the Campo
del Moro from the
Palacio Real*

Madrid

In recent years, Madrid has taken second place to Barcelona – its perennial rival as a city – not just in the spheres of culture and influence, but even on the football field. In 1992, when Madrid was European City of Culture, Barcelona reaped the international rewards of hosting the Olympic Games, but at last the pendulum may be swinging back in the capital's favour, thanks to an ambitious renovation programme that is transforming many of the great museums. The city's chief fascination remains that day-to-day life seems to have altered little, despite growing dynamism since joining the European Union. Archibald Lyall's observation from the 1960s, that Madrid was both the most Spanish and the least Spanish city on the peninsula, still rings true.

> ' ... the least Spanish because it is the most modernised and inter-national, and the most Spanish because ...of the mixed population which has flowed into it from various regions of Spain, it is a synthesis of them all. '
>
> ARCHIBALD LYALL
> *Well Met in Madrid* (1960)

Madrid

Like Piccadilly Circus in London or Times Square in New York, Madrid has its own heartbeat: the Puerta del Sol square. This is the focus of the old city, which is bordered by the Palacio Real to the west and the Paseo del Prado to the east. On this leafy boulevard are the city's three world-famous museums of art.

The northern boundary of the old quarter is the 100-year-old Gran Vía, while around the southern perimeter a loop of broad roads joins the Puerta de Toledo and the Glorieta de los Embajadores. Within this relatively small area are narrow, medieval streets and alleyways, massive churches and a host of bars and restaurants.

Madrid's lungs are to the east and west. Beyond the Prado (► 26) is the Parque del Retiro (► 24) with its formal paths and gardens; beyond the Palacio Real is the Casa de Campo, a vast park with a lake and recreation area. North of the Gran Vía is another network of old streets, including the Chueca district. Usually labelled as Madrid's gay area, this is open to all and has many trendy restaurants. To the northeast, the Salamanca district is Madrid at its most affluent, with expensive apartments and elegant shops overlooking tree-lined streets.

With few skyscrapers, Madrid does not overwhelm the visitor, and as the renovation of old buildings continues, the capital is looking better than ever. It is a compact city, so whether you walk or take the Metro, you can see and do a lot in a relatively short time.

The Casa de la Panadería on the Plaza Mayor

Cool cloisters line the Plaza Mayor

The ornate Basilica de San Miguel

BASILICA DE SAN FRANCISCO EL GRANDE

40A1
Calle de San Buenaventura 1
91 365 38 00
Tue–Fri 11–1, 5–7. Closed public hols
Plenty near by (€)
Puerta de Toledo, La Latina
Ramp
Cheap
Iglesia de San Andrés (➤ 45)
Guided tour only

BASILICA DE SAN MIGUEL

40B2
Calle de San Justo 4
91 548 40 11
Open for mass
Botín (➤ 33)
Sol, Opera
None Free
Plaza Mayor (➤ 25), Casa de la Villa (➤ 36)

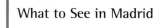

What to See in Madrid

BASILICA DE SAN FRANCISCO EL GRANDE

A long-term restoration programme is underway inside the vast 18th-century church, which stands on the site of a hermitage built by San Francisco (St Francis of Assisi) in 1217. Despite the scaffolding, guides still show you the highlights of a building that has served as a church, national pantheon and even an army barracks. Joseph Bonaparte, the upstart king of Spain, wanted to use it as the parliament building. The enormous dome measures 33m across. In the very first chapel to the left of the main entrance is *The Sermon of San Bernardino of Siena* (1781) by Goya. He produced this unremarkable work at the age of 35, long before the dramatic canvases that are the highlight of the Prado (➤ 26). Even in his early career Goya put himself into his paintings; here he is the one in yellow, on the right-hand side. Behind the altar is the Sala Capitular, with its carved wooden seats and paintings by 17th-century Spanish masters such as Francisco Zurbarán and Alonso Cano.

BASILICA DE SAN MIGUEL

One of Madrid's true baroque churches (1739–49), San Miguel was squeezed on to the small plot of ground that once held the church of San Justo. Architect Santiago Bonavía used several design tricks to give the interior the appearance of more space. In the narrow street, the exterior, with its elegant curved façade, statues and bells, also looks bigger. The consistency of the baroque design reflects Bonavía's Italian roots.

BOTÍN ✪

Peer down the steps leading out of the southwest corner of the Plaza Mayor and you see what is, according to the *Guinness Book of Records*, the oldest restaurant business in the world. The descendants of Jean Botín, a French cook, ran a restaurant near by on the Plaza de Herradores until fire destroyed the premises in the 1940s. The *sobrinos* (cousins) took over the present establishment, which dates back to 1725. Each dining-room reeks with atmosphere. One was the 16th-century *bodega* (wine cellar) and has arched brick walls; the others have dark beams and wall tiles. The focal point is the original *horno de asar* (wood-fired oven), hidden behind well-worn antique ceramic tiles. Although the inn has seen a few changes over the centuries, the oven has always been used to roast or bake meat, such as *cochinillo* (roast suckling pig) and *cordero* (milk-fed lamb). After three hours of slow cooking, the meat is so tender you can cut it with a fork. Legend has it that in 1765, the 19-year-old Goya worked at the original Botín, washing dishes. Almost two centuries later, when Ernest Hemingway dined here, the typically *madrileño* dishes were much the same: stuffed pig's trotters, grilled fish, and *cuajada* (curds). Not much has changed today. This remains as much a place for locals as a shrine for foreign visitors.

🟥 40B3
✉️ Calle de Cuchilleros 17
☎️ 91 366 42 17; www.restaurantebotin.com
🕐 Daily 1–4, 8–12
Ⓜ️ Sol, Tirso de Molina
♿ None
🔁 Plaza Mayor (► 25), Basilica de San Miguel (► 32)
❓ Reservation recommended

Botín is the world's oldest restaurant

CALLE MAYOR

🔲 67E4
🍴 Plenty (€–€€)
Ⓜ Serrano, Núñez de Balboa

Below: *you have to be smart even to go window-shopping on chic Calle de Serrano*

🔲 41E4
✉ Paseo de Recoletos 2
☎ 91 595 48 00
🕐 Exhibitions: Tue–Fri 11–8, Sat 11–7, Sun 11–2
🍴 Snack bar, elegant restaurant in Palacio, with tables in garden (€–€€)
Ⓜ Banco de España
♿ Good
🎟 Free/cheap (exhibitions)
🔁 Palacio de Comunicaciones (► 57), Plaza de la Cibeles (► 62)
❓ Shop sells Latin-American handicrafts

CALLE DE SERRANO

Calle de Serrano is synonymous with 'expensive'. Li Fifth Avenue in New York or Bond Street in London, it *the* place to go shopping for anything beautiful a costly. A broad thoroughfare, Calle de Serrano ru north–south through the elegant Salamanca distric which was laid out in a grid pattern in the late 19 century. Over the years, nearby streets have als sprouted fine shops. Stroll down Calle de Claudio Coell parallel to Serrano, and explore cross streets such Calle de Jorge Juan, Calle de Goya and Calle de Jo Ortega y Gasset, where limousines, their engines tickin over, wait outside designer boutiques.

CASA DE AMÉRICA

In Spanish, the word 'América' tends to refer to Lat America rather than to the USA. Ties between Spain an her former colonies remain strong, and this lively cultu centre celebrates that connection. Since opening in 199 it has hosted a wide range of exhibitions, concerts, film and events reflecting Latin-American culture.

Next door is the elaborately decorated 19th-centu Palacio de Linares. Supposedly haunted, it was the hom of a wealthy financier whose son fell in love with a sho girl. Sent away to England, he returned to Madrid on h father's death. The couple married, but later discovered letter explaining that the girl was the financier's illegitima daughter. Pope León XIII told them that they could rema together but must be chaste. Their unhappy ghosts ar said to inhabit the mansion.

CASA MUSEO DE LOPE DE VEGA ⚫⚫

Author of some 2,000 plays, Lope de Vega (1562–1635) was Spain's greatest playwright, penning an estimated 21 million lines. Capable of reading Latin at five, he wrote his first four-act play at the age of 12. This indefatigable genius also enlisted in the Spanish Navy (the Armada), was personal secretary to four aristocrats and had several wives and many children. Although he decided to become a priest in 1614, this had little effect on his love life. De Vega lived in this house for the last 25 years of his life, and although only a few items are believed to be his, the author's detailed will enabled experts to refurnish the house much as he knew it.

The garden and vegetable patch of this two-storey, half-timbered shrine have been restored to fit a description in one of his poems: two trees, 10 flowers, two vines, an orange tree and a musk rose. Over the front door is the lintel found when cleaning out the well. The inscription reads *Parva propria magna, magna aliena parva* (To me, my small home is big; to me, other people's large homes are small). The guided tours are led by enthusiastic students. As well as finding out about one of Spain's most renowned authors, you also get some idea of everyday life in a well-off family home in the early 17th century. Note the women's sitting-room where cushions are spread on the *estrado*, a small, Moorish-style dais.

- ➕ 41D2
- ✉ Calle Cervantes 11
- ☎ 91 429 92 16
- 🕐 Tue–Fri 9:30–2, Sat 10–2. Closed public hols, Aug
- 🍴 Plenty near by (€)
- Ⓜ Antón Martín
- ♿ None
- 🎫 Cheap, free Sat
- ↔ Iglesia y Convento de las Trinitarias (➤ 46)
- ❓ Guided tour only

Above: *Lope de Vega still haunts his study*

CALLE
MAYOR

Right: *the Casa de
Cisneros on the Plaza
de la Villa*
Below: *door to the Torre
de los Lujanes, Plaza de
la Villa*

🕂 40B3
✉ Plaza de la Villa 5
☎ 91 588 10 00;
　www.munimadrid.es
🅖 Guided tour Mon 5–7
🍴 Plenty near by (€)
🅜 Opera, La Latina
♿ Few
🎟 Free
↔ Plaza Mayor (➤ 25)

🕂 41F3
✉ Calle Alfonso XII 28, Calle
　Felipe IV 13
☎ 91 330 28 00
🍴 Plenty near by (€)

CASA DE LA VILLA　　　😊😊

Madrid's town hall sits on the Plaza de la Villa, which was
Moorish market place in the 10th and 11th centuries.
this cramped square it is difficult to appreciate the spike
towers and handsome façade that are so typical of 17t
century baroque-Castilian style. The balcony overlookir
the Calle Mayor was added in 1789 so that Queen María
Parma could have a better view of the Corpus Chris
procession. Opposite the town hall is the oldest survivir
private house in Madrid, the 15th-century Casa y Torre d
Lujanes. Part Gothic and part Moorish in style, this buildir
is now used by academics. Legend has it that François I
France was imprisoned in the tower after his capture
the Battle of Pavia (1525).

On the south side of the sloping square is the Casa d
Cisneros, built by a relative of the powerful Cardin
Cisneros in 1537. Note the façade, which is decorated
the plateresque style, so-called because the intrica
carving looks like the work of a *platero* (silversmith
Remodelled in the early 1900s, it makes an elegant offic
building for city employees. In the centre of the plaz
stands the great Spanish admiral, the Marqués de Sant
Cruz, victor over the Turks at the Battle of Lepanto (1571
Both the Casa de la Villa and the Casa de Cisneros are on
open to visitors once a week for a guided tour, which
strictly for enthusiasts.

CASÓN DEL BUEN RETIRO　　😊😊😊

Closed since 1997, this building is part of the grand pla
for the massive reorganisation of the Prado (➤ 26). Alon
with the nearby Museo del Ejército (Army Museum), it
the only reminder of the grandeur that was once the Bue
Retiro Palace, built for Philip IV in the 17th century. *Casó*

Banco de España, Retiro
Atocha

Good

Museo del Prado (➤ 26),
Parque del Retiro (➤ 24),
Museo Nacional de Artes
Decorativas (➤ 50)

Check the building
progress on:
www.museoprado.mcu.es

usually means 'big house', but a century ago it was used as a pejorative term to describe the dilapidated structure. When this part of the Prado art complex reopens, it will house 19th-century art.

Above and left: Casón del Buen Retiro

CATEDRAL DE SAN ISIDRO ★

Calle de Toledo is the busy street leading south from the Plaza Mayor. Although it is narrow, you cannot miss the bulky twin towers of this cathedral, designed to emphasise the importance of the church that is dedicated to Madrid's patron saint. Built between 1622 and 1633, the interior is in the shape of a cross, with the dome above the transept. After Carlos III expelled the Jesuits in 1767, he commissioned the noted architect Ventura Rodríguez to remodel the gloomy interior. For over 200 years, the remains of San Isidro and Santa María de la Cabeza, his equally holy wife, have been venerated here. The faithful also make their way to the third chapel to the right of the main entrance and its figure of Christ carrying the cross. Filing around the statue, they touch the exposed rear heel and bless themselves.

40C2

Calle de Toledo 37

91 369 20 37

Mon–Sat 7:30–1,
6:30–8:30, Sun, public
hols 9–2, 5:30–8:30

Plenty near by (€)

La Latina, Tirso de Molina

None

Free

Plaza Mayor (➤ 25),
Botín (➤ 33)

Above and above right:
Centro Cultural Conde Duque

CENTRO CULTURAL CONDE DUQUE

It is worth checking the entertainment listings to se what is on at this handsome cultural centre. From th outside, all you see is a long brick wall, but step throug the main entrance and doorways labelled *Cuarto a Banderas* (Flag Room) and *Cuerpo de Guardia* (Guar Room) are clues to the building's past. An enormou complex, it was once the barracks for the roya bodyguard, and reflected the grandeur of Felipe V' Palacio Real to the south. Begun in 1720, it house soldiers for 150 years and, despite a fire in the 19t century, its sheer size is still impressive.

Today, it is an important part of Madrid's cultural scene holding special events and exhibitions throughout the yea Most atmospheric is the *Veranos de la Villa* summe festival, staged outdoors in the massive Patio Centra (inner courtyard). From late June to mid-September, th vigorous international programme offers dance, musi singing, theatre and opera.

CONVENTO DE LAS CARBONERAS

It is difficult to find this convent. From Plaza de la Vill step into Calle del Codo and the door is on the right. Th nuns belong to a closed order known as the Carbonera (coal cellars), because their painting of the Virgi Mary was found in a coal cellar. The convent is bette known in Madrid for selling home-made *dulce* (biscuits). This tradition dates back to the 16th centur when Santa Teresa of Avila distributed treats made fror sugar and egg yolk to the poor. Ring a bell for service; a elaborate serving hatch ensures that the privacy of th nuns is not disturbed.

CALLE MAYOR

DID YOU KNOW?

A 200-year-old custom centres on St Anthony, 'the matchmaker'. His feast day on 13 June draws unmarried women to the Ermita. Standing before the baptismal font, each drops 13 pins into the water, presses her palm down and then lifts it out. Each pin sticking to the skin represents a suitor.

ERMITA DE SAN ANTONIO DE LA FLORIDA ✪✪✪

There are two small churches here: the one on the left is a replica, built to hold services. On the right is the original *ermita*, now a museum dedicated to Goya, one of Spain's greatest artists. The ceiling he painted, revolutionary in technique and subject matter, was a turning point in the history of art.

Goya was 52 when he began this project in 1798. He had just recovered from a severe illness that left him deaf, but worked from August to mid-December, using brushes, sponges and even his thumbs to portray St Anthony raising a murdered man from the dead. Use the handy mirrors to study the characters: St Anthony, the victim and the man falsely accused of the crime – the saint's own father. This is not an idealised scene with important nobles and ecclesiastics; these are real people showing real emotions, wearing ordinary clothes. It's easy to imagine how this painting shocked the establishment at the time.

➕ 66A3
✉ Glorieta de San Antonio de la Florida 5
☎ 91 542 07 22
🕐 Tue–Fri 10–2, 4–8, Sat, Sun 10–2. Closed public hols
🍴 Casa Mingo (next door) (€)
Ⓜ Príncipe Pío
♿ None
💶 Cheap (free during restoration work)
↔ Teleférico (➤ 71)
❓ Free guided tours (Spanish, English) Sat 11, 12

Goya's remains are buried in front of the altar in the Ermita de San Antonio de la Florida

CALLE
MAYOR

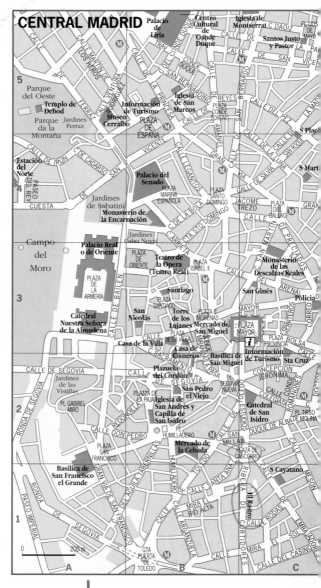

CENTRAL MADRID

Palacio de Liria
Centro Cultural de Conde Duque
Iglesia de Montserrat
Santos Justo y Pastor

Parque del Oeste
Templo de Debod
Jardines Ferraz
Información de Turismo
Museo Cerralbo
Iglesia de San Marcos

Estación del Norte

Parque da la Montaña
Palacio del Senado
Jardines de Sabatini
Monasterio de la Encarnación
Jardines Cabo Noval

Campo del Moro
Palacio Real o de Oriente
Teatro de la Opera (Teatro Real)
Monasterio de las Descalzas Reales

Catedral Nuestra Señora de la Almudena
Santiago
San Ginés
Policía
San Nicolás
Torre de los Lujanes
Mercado de San Miguel
Casa de la Villa

Casa de Cisneros
Basílica de San Miguel
Información de Turismo
Sta Cruz

Plazuela del Cordón
San Pedro el Viejo
Iglesia de San Andrés y Capilla de San Isidro
Catedral de San Isidro

Jardines de las Vistillas
Mercado de la Cebada

Basílica de San Francisco el Grande
S Cayatano

El Rastro

0   200 m

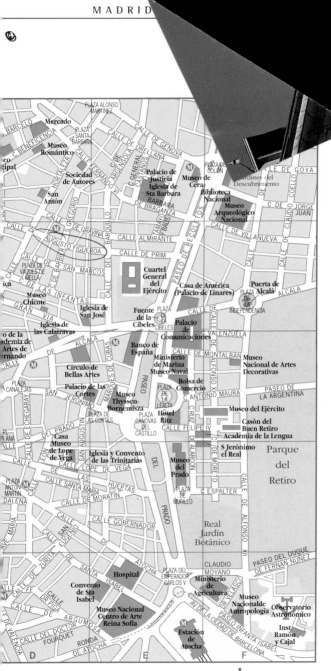

Medieval Madrid

CALLE
MAYOR

*Start at the Plaza Mayor
(➤ 25). The steps at the
southwest corner lead to the
Calle de los Cuchilleros, with
its centuries-old mesones
(taverns). Cross Plaza de la
Puerta Cerrada to Calle de
la Cava Baja.*

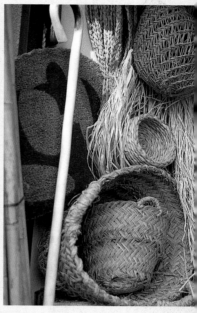

At No 9, La Posada de la Villa dates
back to 1642. This quarter retains its
historic atmosphere, with tiny shops
that still sell basketware and *alpargatas* (rope-soled sandals). At the
end, across the Plaza del
Humilladero, on the right, is the
huge dome of Iglesia de San Andrés
(➤ 45).

*Walk round the south side
and into the Plaza de la
Paja.*

Once the main square of the
medieval city, this was overlooked
by a royal palace. Today, a lone statue sits on a bench
reading the paper.

*At the bottom of the square turn right along
Calle del Príncipe de Anglona to the 15th-
century Iglesia de San Pedro el Viejo, marked by
a 14th-century mudéjar (Moorish) tower. Turn
left on Travesía del Nuncio and right onto Calle
de Segovia.*

A plaque at No 1 records the birthplace of San Isidro,
Madrid's patron saint. Turn immediately left on Calle del
Doctor Letamendi, past the Basilica de San Miguel (➤ 32),
along Calle de Puñonrostro and Calle del Codo. Pass the
Convento de las Carboneras on the left (➤ 38). Continue
to the town hall, the Casa de la Villa (➤ 36).

*Turn right, walk back along the Calle Mayor to
the Plaza Mayor.*

*Basketware shop on the
Calle de la Cava*

Distance
2km

Time
Half a day with stops

Start/end point
Plaza Mayor
✚ 40C3
Ⓢ Sol

Lunch
Posada de la Villa (€–€€)
✉ Calle de la Cava Baja 9
☎ 91 366 18 60/91
366 18 80

Opposite: *the 17th-
century Casa de la Villa
(town hall) was designed
by Gomez de Mora*

43

⊞ 28B3
✉ Paseo de la Castellana
144
☎ 91 398 43 32 (stadium),
91 457 06 79 (museum);
www.realmadrid.com
◷ Regular matches during
football season
🍴 Restaurant/café (€)
Ⓢ Santiago Bernabéu
♿ Good
✋ Cheap (museum)
❓ Museum (gate 5) open
Tue–Sun 10–7:30

ESTADIO SANTIAGO BERNABÉU (BERNABÉU STADIUM) ✪✪

Madrid may be crowded with churches, but the most popular modern shrine is this football stadium – the home of Real Madrid. Set on a broad boulevard, with its own Metro station, the 86,000-seat stadium hosted the 1982 World Cup Final. Founded in 1902, 'Real' became one of the most famous football clubs in the world. The name means Royal, and the club has proved to be a dynastic force in football, so much so that in 1998, FIFA, the world governing body, awarded them the accolade, 'the best club in the history of football'.

Even if you can't get to a game, you can experience the atmosphere by visiting the museum, right across from the Metro exit. Crammed with dazzling silver trophies and resonating with screams of '*Gol!, Gol!, Gol!*' this is a football fan's paradise. Numerous video screens show clips from great matches of the past, including their nine European Cup triumphs between 1956 and 2002, as well as 17 Spanish Cups and 28 Spanish league championships. The oldest trophy dates from 1905, but the most spectacular is one that looks like a fort. Standing 1.6m high, it weighs 75kg, 25kg of which are solid silver. Success is not limited to football: Real, like many Spanish football clubs, participates in many sports. Their basketball team, for example, has an equally glowing history, having won eight European Cups plus the 1981 world club title.

DID YOU KNOW?

Real Madrid are known as the *merengues* (meringues) because of their all-white strip. Rivals Atlético Madrid are the *colchoneros* (mattress makers) because of their red and white striped shirts.

Steve McManaman of Real Madrid in action against Numantia in 1999

IGLESIA DE LAS CALATRAVAS ✪

In the 17th and 18th centuries the most important street in Madrid was the Calle de Alcalá, which led to the university town of Alcalá de Henares. Facing today's traffic and hemmed in by office blocks, this church is all that is left of the original 17th-century convent of the military order of the Comendadoras of Calatrava, founded by the wives of knights who joined the Crusades. Topped by a fine dome, the massive pink-brick exterior is covered in ornate sculpture. The interior is even more opulent. Here, the focal point (if you can see it in the gloomy light) is the massive altarpiece of José Churriguera, the sculptor who lent his name to an exuberant baroque decorative style – Churrigueresque.

✚ 41D3
✉ Calle de Alcalá 25
☎ 91 521 80 35
🕐 Mornings and 7:30PM for mass, most days
🍴 Círculo de Bellas Artes (opposite) (€)
🚇 Sevilla
♿ None
🎟 Free
↔ Museo de la Real Academia de Bellas Artes de San Fernando (➤ 51)

Above: *Iglesia de las Calatra*

IGLESIA DE SAN ANDRÉS APÓSTOL ✪

San Andrés is a church with two significant chapels. San Andrés itself, occupying the domed end of the building, reopened in 1998 after years of renovation. Compared with the poorly-lit interiors of most churches, this one is a surprise: bright pink and grey, highlighted with fruit, flowers and angels, like the marzipan on an expensive cake. At the back of San Andrés is the Capilla de San Isidro, which once held the bones of San Isidro, Madrid's patron saint. Beneath the church, renovation continues on the 16th-century Capilla del Obispo (Bishop's Chapel). Closed to the public, it contains one of the most magnificent Gothic altarpieces in Madrid, a towering, gilded masterpiece attributed to Francisco Giralte.

✚ 40B2
✉ Plaza de San Andrés 1
☎ 91 365 48 71
🕐 Mon–Sat 8–1, 5:30–7:30, Sun 9–2
🍴 Plenty near by (€)
🚇 La Latina
♿ None
🎟 Free
↔ Catedral de San Isidro (➤ 37), Basílica de San Francisco el Grande (➤ 32)

CALLE MAYOR

+ 40B5
⊠ Calle San Leonardo 10
☎ 91 547 10 79
🕐 Mass 8–12, 8PM
🍴 Plenty near by (€)
🚇 Plaza de España/Ventura Rodríguez
♿ None
👛 Free
↔ Centro Cultural Conde Duque (➤ 38), Museo Cerralbo (➤ 54)

IGLESIA DE SAN MARCOS ✪

The nearby Ventura Rodríguez Metro station is a tribute to the flamboyant architect of this small, mid-18th-century baroque church. This was an early work by Ventura Rodríguez, who went on design the chapel in the Palacio Real (➤ 23). Dusty and dull on the outside, the cream interior is fresh and bright, with an impressive and massive altarpiece by Juan de Mena. In the cupola, the fine frescoes by Luis González Velázquez depict the dashing Duke of Berwick astride a white horse. He was the hero of the Battle of Almansa (1707), a crucial victory in the War of the Spanish Succession, which placed the first of the Bourbon kings on the Spanish throne. The 18th-century organ is still in working order.

+ 41D2
⊠ Calle de Lope de Vega 18
☎ 91 429 56 71
🕐 Mon–Fri 8:30AM, Sat 7PM, Sun 9:30AM, 11:30AM
🍴 Plenty near by (€)
🚇 Antón Martín
♿ None
👛 Free
↔ Casa Museo Lope de Vega (➤ 35)

IGLESIA Y CONVENTO DE LAS TRINITARIAS ✪

The Trinitarias, who wear white cassocks marked with a bold red and blue cross, are a closed order of nuns. In their 17th-century church a plaque commemorates the burial place of Cervantes, author of *Don Quixote*. Each year on 23 April, a memorial service for Spain's most famous writer is held by Spain's Academy of Language. Authors Lope de Vega, Luis de Góngora and Francisco de Quevedo also lived near by and worshipped here. Although the church has fine paintings and a grand altarpiece, the appeal here is to follow in the footsteps of these literary giants. Visiting hours are limited to half an hour before mass, but you are not required to stay for the service itself.

+ 40B3
⊠ Plaza de San Miguel
☎ 91 548 12 14
🕐 Mon–Fri 9–2, 5–8, Sat 9–2
🍴 Café del Mercado (€)
🚇 Sol
♿ None
👛 Free
↔ Plaza Mayor (➤ 25), Casa de la Villa (➤ 36)

MERCADO DE SAN MIGUEL ✪

This is the only traditional food market of its kind left in the heart of Madrid. Built in 1915 but recently renovated, the hall is a graceful combination of green-painted iron and glass. Even if you are not buying, a stroll past the stalls shows why Madrid is called Spain's biggest port: all the best freshly caught fish is transported straight to the capital. Fishmongers might be working on a

whole *mero* (halibut) weighing 40kg; *charcuterías* (delicatessens) are piled with dozens of types of sausage and cheese; *carnicerías* (butchers) offer tender pork; and the range of colourful fresh fruit and vegetables is astonishing. Stop for a snack at the small café-bar in the middle and eavesdrop on vendors discussing deals.

In Madrid terms, this marketplace is relatively new. It dates back to the early 19th century, when José I demolished narrow streets, old houses and ancient churches to create new squares and open spaces in the capital. His enthusiasm earned him the nickname, *El Rey Plazuelas* (King of the Little Squares). The San Miguel market replaced a church of the same name.

Left: *Madrid is jokingly known as Spain's main fishing port*

Food, glorious food, at the Mercado de San Miguel

CALLE MAYOR

The Monasterio de la Encarnación is crammed with treasures

MONASTERIO DE LAS DESCALZAS REALES
(➤ 16, TOP TEN)

MONASTERIO DE LA ENCARNACIÓN ⚫⚫

Another of Madrid's closed orders dedicated to the royal family, this convent is famous on two counts: its collection of some 4,000 *relicarios* (reliquaries) and an annual miracle. Whether you believe that the reliquaries contain the authentic bones of saints or a fragment of the true cross depends on your religious persuasion. However, according to the curator, visitors should appreciate the reliquaries as works of art, created as expressions of religious belief during the 17th century – Spain's Golden Age.

The reliquaries are preserved in glass cases, which line the walls of what looks like a heavily decorated library with an impressive, gilded altar. They come in all shapes and sizes in precious materials of the period, such as coral, marble and crystal, as well as gold and silver. The designs reflect the talents of artists, not just from Spain but also from Germany, the Netherlands, Italy and even the Orient. One of the most venerated reliquaries is a small vial containing a droplet of blood, which is reputedly from the 4th-century physician and martyr, San Pantaleón. On 26 July, the eve of the saint's feast day, the vial is placed on the altar of the church in the convent. There, according to the faithful, *la sangre* (the blood) rematerialises. The convent, still home to a small community of nuns, was founded in 1611 by Margarita of Austria, wife of Felipe III. Although the handsome façade is original, architect Ventura Rodríguez remodelled the interior after a fire in the 18th century.

🔲 40B4
✉ Plaza de la Encarnación 1
☎ 91 542 00 59
🕐 Tue–Sat 10:30–12:45, 4–5:45, Sun, public hols 11–1:45. Closed Fri PM, Mon and Aug
🍴 Plenty near by (€)
🚇 Opera
♿ None
🎫 Cheap; free Wed
↔ Palacio Real (➤ 23)
❓ Joint ticket available with the nearby Monasterio de las Descalzas Reales (➤ 16)

DID YOU KNOW?

Napoleon Bonaparte put his brother, Joseph, on the throne of Spain in 1808. This precipitated the Madrid uprising against the French on the *2 de mayo* (2 May). Never accepted, José's only popular measure was the relaxation of duty on alcohol, which won him the nickname *Pepe Botella* (Joe Bottle).

MUSEO DE AMÉRICA (➤ 17, TOP TEN)

MUSEO ARQUEOLÓGICO NACIONAL ✪
The National Archaeological Museum's collection reflects Mediterranean cultures as well as those of the Iberian peninsula. Although the old-fashioned, glass-cased displays could put off the younger generation, exhibits such as the *Dama de Elche* are fascinating. Discovered near Alicante, this finely-carved bust of a noblewoman from Elche dates from around the 4th century BC; the hole at the back probably held the ashes of a well-born person. Like a photograph in *Vogue* magazine, her elaborate headdress and jewellery reflect the fashions of Iberia, but they also relate to Greek and Celtic styles. Moreover, they can be traced through the centuries to the traditional hairstyles of Valencia. Other treasures in the museum include porcelain from the Buen Retiro factory, Greek pottery, and an intriguing Roman sundial. In the garden, a specially dugout underground room contains reproductions of the famous prehistoric cave paintings of bison and deer from Altamira. Explanations in several languages are available.

MUSEO NACIONAL DE ANTROPOLOGÍA ✪
This would be dull were it not for the quirky objects on display. School children rush to the ghoulish Room III, to the left of the main entrance, to see the skeleton of the *Gigante Extremeño*, Spain's tallest man. Agustín Luengo Capilla, who died in 1849, aged 26, was an astonishing 2.35m tall. Most of the building is devoted to tribal relics: big gods and little gods, wooden shields and dug-out canoes. Other children's favourites include Brazilian feathered head-dresses and gruesome shrunken heads dangling in a glass case.

✚ 41F5
✉ Calle del Serrano 13
☎ 91 577 79 12/91 577 79 19/20; www.man.es
🕐 Tue–Sat 9:30–8:30, Sun, public hols 9:30–2:30
🍴 Plenty near by (€)
Ⓜ Serrano, Colón
♿ Good
🎟 Cheap; free under-18, over-65, Sat after 2:30, Sun
↔ Calle de Serrano (➤ 34)

Above: *inside the Museo Arqueológico Nacional*

✚ 67E1
✉ Calle Alfonso XII 68
☎ 91 530 64 18/91 539 59 95; www.mcu.es/ nmuseos/antropologia
🕐 Tue–Sat 10–7:30, Sun, public hols 10–2
🍴 Plenty near by (€)
Ⓜ Atocha, Atocha RENFE
♿ Few   ✋ Cheap
↔ Real Fábrica de Tapices (➤ 70)

49

CALLE MAYOR

🔳 41F3
✉ Calle de Montalbán 12
☎ 91 532 64 99
🕐 Tue–Fri 9:30–3, Sat, Sun, public hols 10–2
🍴 Plenty near by (€)
Ⓜ Banco de España, Retiro
♿ Good
💰 Cheap
↔ Parque del Retiro (➤ 24)
❓ Free tour Sun 11:30 (not Jul–Sep)

MUSEO NACIONAL DE ARTES DECORATIVAS ✪✪

Like London's Victoria and Albert Museum and the Musée des Arts Decoratifs in Paris, this is a must for anyone interested in design and fine craftsmanship. Throughout the five floors of this converted mansion the collection focuses on Spanish traditions, but places them in a wider context. The glassware from La Granja, for example, contrasts with centuries-old pieces dating from Greek and Roman times as well as more modern Lalique. Porcelain from Spanish factories compares with works from elsewhere in Europe, such as Meissen, Limoges and Sèvres.

The undoubted highlight is the famous tiled kitchen on the fourth floor, brought here from a palace in Valencia. Covered in hand-painted pictorial tiles, this is a snapshot of 18th-century life that shows the mistress of the house and her retinue of servants – from the butler in frock coat and buckled shoes to the African woman wielding a broom. Food historians note the copper pots, the leg of lamb, partridge, *chorizos* (sausages) and even a tray of cakes and *turrón* (nougat) that look good enough to eat. Most fun are

CALLE MAYOR

the cats which are stealing a fish from the pan and an eel from the shopping basket.

Furniture, tapestries, an ornate silver tabletop showing all the signs of the zodiac – there is much to admire here. Don't, however, miss the room dedicated to the fan, that most Spanish of all fashion accessories. Follow its evolution from simple palm leaves to intricate designs in silk and mother-of-pearl. Even the language of the fan is deciphered.

MUSEO NACIONAL CENTRO DE ARTE REINA SOFÍA
(► 19, TOP TEN)

MUSEO DE LA REAL ACADEMIA ✪✪✪
DE BELLAS ARTES DE SAN FERNANDO
Both Picasso and Dalí studied at the grand, but grim-looking Royal Academy, the oldest museum in the city (1752). Climb the sombre, massive stone steps; once inside the gallery, all is brightly-lit. This uncrowded museum has a serendipitous charm. Although Goya's paintings are at the end of the itinerary, don't rush there

but take your time to discover Francisco Zurbarán's powerful portraits of monks, which dominate Room 6, and Reubens' *Susana y Los Viejos* (Susanna and the Elders), the highlight of Room 13. There are curiosities galore, such as Giuseppe Archimboldo's curious painting in Room 14. Called *La Primavera* (Spring), this is a portrait concocted from daisies, wild strawberries, roses and iris. Two contrasting portraits of famous generals, Napoleon Bonaparte and George Washington, dominate Room 35. The French emperor seems to be wearing a dress, while the American holds a map of the capital named after him.

Find Joaquín Sorolla (► 20) and Juan Gris among a mish-mash of modern Spanish artists in Rooms 25 and 29. Room 20 is popular for its famous but surprisingly small Goya painting, *El Entierro de la Sardina* (The Burial of the Sardine), depicting this rather bizarre local custom. Other works by Goya in the room include self-portraits, as well as sketches for the famous oils of scenes in a mad house, of the Inquisition and of penitents.

🕂 41D3
✉ Calle de Alcalá 13
☎ 91 524 08 64
🕐 Tue–Fri 9–7, Sat–Mon, public hols 10–2
🍴 Plenty near by (€)
Ⓜ Sevilla, Sol
♿ None
💶 Cheap; free under-18, over-65, Sat, Sun

Statues adorn the Museo de Bellas Artes

The Gran Vía

CALLE MAYOR

Start in the Plaza de España.

Statues of author Miguel de Cervantes and his characters, Don Quixote and Sancho Panza, dominate the square. The two tallest structures, the Edificio España and the Torre de Madrid, were designed and built by the prolific Otamendi brothers in the early 1950s.

Walk southeast down the Gran Vía.

When Madrid expanded in the early 1900s, over 300 houses and 14 ancient streets were demolished to make way for this boulevard. New buildings, some inspired by the North American skyscraper, include 1920s–30s cinemas, such as the Capitol in the Carrión building (Gran Vía 41) and the Cine Callao (Plaza del Callao 3). The Palacio de la Prensa (Plaza del Callao 4) originally provided office workers with everything from entertainment to shops and restaurants, all under one roof.

Continue east along the Gran Vía.

At Gran Vía 28 is the Telefónica (► 71). This American-designed skyscraper (1929) was the tallest in the city for some 25 years. From here on, buildings are older and more heavily decorated. Note the extravagant rooftop embellishments of the 1913 Edificio del Banco Central (Gran Vía 18) and the Edificios La Estrella (Gran Vía 7 and 10). No 7 shows a Moorish influence. The walk ends at the Parisian-style Edificio Metrópolis, which is crowned by a statue of Winged Victory. Down at street level, the figure of a violet seller commemorates the street vendors whose flowers once heralded spring in the city.

Distance
1.3km

Time
3 hours including visits

Start point
Plaza de España
🚇 40B5
Ⓜ Plaza de España

End point
Corner of Gran Vía and Calle de Alcalá
🚇 41D4
Ⓜ Banco de España

Lunch
Museo del Jamón (€)
✉ Gran Vía 72
☎ 91 541 20 23

Two views of the Gran Vía

METROPOLIS

CALLE MAYOR

🔲 40A5
✉ Calle Ventura Rodríguez 17
☎ 91 547 36 46/7
🕐 Tue–Sat 9:30–2:30, Sun 10–2; Jul, Aug 10–2, Sun 10–1:30
🍴 Plenty (€)
🚇 Plaza de España, Ventura Rodríguez
♿ Few
🎟 Cheap, free Wed, Sun
↔ Iglesia de San Marcos (➤ 46)

MUSEO CERRALBO ⭐

The 17th Marquis of Cerralbo (1845–1922) was passionate about politics and the arts. His collection, which has to be shown as he left it, includes 30,000 'works of art, archaeological objects and curios', gathered from around the world. Although the best-known of his paintings is The Ecstasy of St Francis of Assisi by El Greco, there is also porcelain, Greek and Roman pottery, furniture, swords and oriental armour. Connoisseurs appreciate the aristocratic mansion as much as the artefacts. The sumptuous ballroom (renovated in 1999) contrasts with the practical office-library; even the parquet floors in the dining room and billiard room demand admiration.

> ### DID YOU KNOW?
>
> The ancient Burial of the Sardine ceremony painted by Goya (➤ 51) is still an annual event. On Ash Wednesday, a mock funeral procession – bearing a tiny coffin and accompanied by a jazz band – makes its way from the Ermita de San Antonio de la Florida (➤ 39) to the Los Pajaritos fountain in the Casa de Campo, where the sardine is interred.

🔲 41D4
✉ Gran Vía 12
☎ 91 532 67 37
🕐 Mon–Thu 5PM–12AM, Fri, Sat 5PM–3AM
🚇 Gran Vía
♿ None
🎟 Free
↔ Telefónica

MUSEO CHICOTE ⭐

Not a museum, but a cocktail bar! Founded in 1931 by Perico Chicote to 'mix drinks, lives and opinions', this art deco bar survives more on memories than present-day glamour. Photos of Frank Sinatra, Salvador Dalí, Bette Davis and Ernest Hemingway line the walls, but as to who sat where and when, that depends on which waiter you ask. Chicote's museum of odd drinks and bottles has gone, but madrileños still come late for a cocktail, and at weekends it's the busiest museum in town – after midnight that is.

🔲 41F3
✉ Calle de Méndez Núñez 1
☎ 91 522 89 77
🕐 Tue–Sun 10–2
🍴 Plenty near by (€)
🚇 Banco de España, Retiro
♿ None
🎟 Cheap, Sat free
↔ Museo del Prado (➤ 26), Parque del Retiro (➤ 24)

MUSEO DEL EJÉRCITO ⭐

This imposing building, part of the former Palacio del Buen Retiro, is part of the grand expansion scheme of the Prado (➤ 26). For art historians, the opulent Antigua Salón de los Reinos (the throne room) holds particular significance. To add to the pomp, Velázquez was commissioned to paint 12 vast canvases celebrating battles won by Felipe IV, while Zurbarán created the 10 Labours of Hercules. The eccentric Army Museum that has filled the room in recent years will soon be moved to the Alcázar in Toledo to make way for the Prado's collection of 17th-century paintings.

CALLE
MAYOR

MUSEO LÁZARO GALDIANO (▶ 18, TOP TEN)

MUSEO NAVAL ✪

You need a working knowledge of Spanish or naval history to get the best out of this small museum. This is a pity, since Spain's maritime power changed the course of world events. In addition to numerous models of boats, there are vivid paintings depicting naval victories. A famous battle prize is the flag of the French battleship *L'Atlas* (Room VII). Napoleon presented ensigns to all his commanders before the Battle of Trafalgar in 1805 – this is the only one to survive. Don't miss Room XVII, where the routes of Spain's explorers are plotted on a world map covering an entire wall. Here, too, is the first map of the New World by a cartographer who had actually been there. Dated 1500, it was made by Juan de la Cosa, captain of the *Santa María*, one of the trio of ships led by Columbus in 1492.

MUSEO DEL PRADO (▶ 26, TOP TEN)

➕ 67D2
✉ Paseo del Prado 5
☎ 91 379 52 99
🕐 Tue–Sun 10–2
🍴 Plenty near by (€)
🚇 Banco de España
♿ None
✋ Free

Above: *star parade: the bar at Museo Chicote*

San Gregorio Magno, *painted by Goya, in the Museo Romántico chapel*

🚩 67D4
✉ Calle de San Mateo 13
☎ 91 448 10 45
🕐 Tue–Sat 9–3, Sun, public hols 10–2. Closed Aug
🍴 Plenty near by (€)
Ⓜ Tribunal, Alonso Martínez
♿ Ramp, elevator
💷 Cheap, free Sun
❓ Due to re-open in 2003 after renovations

MUSEO ROMÁNTICO ⚡

Millions of visitors to Spain should be grateful to the Marqués de la Vega-Inclán (1858–1942). He set up the country's tourist infrastructure and initiated the *paradores* the national group of hotels in former castles and monasteries. His collection of 19th-century paintings, books and furniture formed the nucleus of this somewhat eccentric museum, which is dedicated to artists and writers of a romantic bent.

Start by paying your respects to the marquis, whose portrait by the Spanish painter, Joaquín Sorolla (► 20) hangs among family memorabilia in a small study to the left of the entrance. Continuing through the 25 rooms, little seems to have changed in the 75 years since the museum first opened its doors. In the grand ballroom (Room 4), the carpet from the Real Fábrica de Tapices (► 70) measures 11m by 6m. Next door are two examples of 19th century Spanish Romantic art: an imposing portrait of General Prim, leader of the Spanish Revolution of 1868 and gruesome portrayals of ways to commit suicide - considered 'romantic' at the time. The choices illustrated include death by pistol, sword, dagger or jumping off a cliff. The most extreme of all Spain's romantics was Mariano José de Larra, who committed suicide using the pistols that are on display in Room 17. Arguably, the only work of real quality in the whole collection is *San Gregorio Magno*, a large canvas by Goya in the *oratorio* (private chapel).

MUSEO SOROLLA (► 20, TOP TEN)

MUSEO THYSSEN-BORNEMISZA (► 22, TOP TEN)

PALACIO DE COMUNICACIONES ✪✪

Looking like a palace on the outside and a train station within, this building could well be the world's most impressive post office. Nicknamed Nuestra Señora de las Communicaciones, as if it were a cathedral, it dominates the Plaza de la Cibeles (➤ 62). The Banco de España stands opposite; further south, on the Paseo del Prado, is the Stock Exchange. These three grandiose buildings from the beginning of the 20th century were part of the city's programme of expansion and reflect a confidence in Madrid's future.

Inside, the post office is all marble and brass beneath a stained-glass ceiling providing plenty of natural light. The 80 different counters offer a wide variety of services from posting a parcel to paying the rent. Buying a stamp seems mundane by comparison. In the two side wings, you can stand and write your postcards at one of the 44 desks. Outside, customers slip their mail into 12 brass *buzones* (post boxes) marked Madrid, Sevilla, Valencia, Barcelona and more. There is even a special one for *urgentes*. The post office is open daily; when the main door is closed at weekends use Gate H. Within the 12,000sq m complex is a chapel for members of staff (Door Y) and the Museo Postal y de Telecomunicación, at the side (Door M) on Calle de Montalbán. This has been revamped to show off one of the world's great stamp collections. The oldest stamp, from 1850, bears the face of Isabel II.

➕ 41E3
✉ Plaza de la Cibeles s/n
☎ 91 521 65 00; Museum 91 396 26 79
🕐 daily 8AM–9.30PM; (Museum) Mon–Fri 9–2, 4–7, Sat 9–2
🍴 Plenty near by (€)
Ⓜ Banco de España
♿ Few
ℹ Free; museum free with passport/ID
↔ Casa de América (➤ 34), Museo Naval (➤ 55), Plaza de la Cibeles (➤ 62)

The grand main post office, the Palacio de Comunicaciones

CALLE MAYOR

The home of the Spanish parliament, the Palacio de las Cortes

---

🗺 41D3
✉ Plaza de las Cortes s/n
☎ 91 390 60 00
🕐 Sat 10:30–1, guided tour only. Closed Aug, public hols
🍴 Plenty near by (€)
Ⓜ Sevilla
♿ Good
🎟 Free
↔ Museo Thyssen-Bornemisza (➤ 22)
❓ Official ID (such as a passport) required, free booklet given out

PALACIO DE LAS CORTES   ✪✪

The events of 23 February 1981 marked a turning point in Spanish history. Civil Guard commander Colonel Tejero entered the *Salón de Sesiones* in the parliament building, firing his pistol and ordering delegates to the floor. Television cameras relayed the action live to a shocked country and for a while it looked as if Spain might revert to military dictatorship. Discussion of those events are the prime topic during the 45-minute tours of this neo-classical mid-19th century building. First, however, you pass through four rooms as the guide describes the ornate paintings, chandeliers and furniture. There are portraits of 19th-century politicians and an intriguing 3m-high clock that registers the weather and humidity, as well as the date and time. Spaniards study the seven constitutions of Spain – from the earliest (1812), to the current one issued in 1978 and signed by Juan Carlos.

The highlight, however, is the deputies' chamber with its 350 leather armchairs. The order of seating for the cabinet reflects the seniority of the ministry; two panels show how individual members vote: *sí, no* or *abs*. But what Spaniards of all ages want to know is, 'where are the bullet holes?' Even bored teenagers pay attention as the guide points out the 40 punctures in the walls and ceiling. Parents recall those momentous hours when tanks threatened Valencia, and Spain waited to see whether or not the new democracy would survive.

PALACIO REAL (➤ 23, TOP TEN)

PARQUE DEL RETIRO (➤ 24, TOP TEN)

THE PASEOS ⭐⭐

Madrid is split down the middle, from north to south, by a series of *paseos* or boulevards: the Paseo de la Castellana (4km), the Paseo de Recoletos (1km) and the Paseo del Prado (1.5km, Walk ➤ 69). These are interspersed by grand roundabouts, often graced by imposing statues and fountains, such as the Plaza de la Cibeles (➤ 62).

Most visitors enjoy the stretch of the Paseo del Prado linking the three great art museums: the Prado (➤ 26), the Museo Nacional Centro de Arte Reina Sofía (➤ 19) and the Museo Thyssen-Bornemisza (➤ 22). Trees shade strollers along the eastern side of this *paseo*, which borders the Real Jardín Botánico (➤ 70).

The Paseo de Recoletos has echoes of Paris, with its glamorous cafés. The most famous is the Gran Café Gijón (➤ 99), known as a meeting place for writers and artists in the 1920s. Today, actors, agents and directors still meet to read scripts and clinch deals. In the evenings a pianist tinkles away.

The Paseo de la Castellana, which cuts through the modern part of the city, is lined with imposing office blocks and, to the north, the Estadio Santiago Bernabéu, home of Real Madrid football club (➤ 44). In summer, the Castellana is known for its *terrazas* (open-air cafés), which open late and close in the early hours. Locals have their favourite *terraza* where they meet to chat and drink, often to a background of music.

Botero's hand sculpture on the Paseo de la Castellana

Coffee break at the Café El Espejo on the Paseo de Recoletos

Food & Drink

Madrileños are a sociable people for whom eating and drinking in bars and restaurants is a way of life. They tend to enjoy traditional dishes made from fresh, full-flavoured ingredients, often prepared quite simply.

Tapas *come in a hundred different shapes and tastes*

Try Madrid-style cooking, then sample the cuisines from all the regions of Spain, from the Basque country to Galicia, and from Asturias to Valencia. Portions are usually hearty and prices reasonable.

In fact, the only disappointments could come when ordering non-Spanish dishes, catering for 'international' tastes.

Desserts, however, tend to be standard and unadventurous. They include the ubiquitous *flan* (crème caramel), *arroz con leche* (rice pudding) and *manzana asada* (baked apple).

Fish & Meat Dishes

Madrid is often called Spain's main fishing port because the fleets send the best of their catch straight to the city. Sauces are rarely needed for the thick slices of *lubina* (John Dory), *besugo* (sea bass) and *ventresca* (tuna), which are grilled *a la plancha* (on a hot plate). Basque restaurants are particularly well known for their fish dishes, which have relatively simple sauces, such as white wine with garlic and parsley. The Spanish are also great meat eaters, choosing between tender pork, *chuletas de lechal* (lamb chops) and chunks of *solomillo* (sirloin steak). There is also a vast array of sausages, from *chorizos* (spicy pork) to *morcilla* (black pudding).

Madrid's own dish is *cocido madrileño*, a stew of meat and vegetables that traditionally is prepared in an earthenware pot by the fire. Lamb and suckling pig are roasted slowly in wood-fired ovens, until the meat is so tender that it falls off the bone.

Snacks

Don't miss *tapas*, the little snacks that are eaten throughout the day, but especially in the late afternoon and

early evening before restaurants open for dinner. A *tapa* was once a small round slice of bread set on top of your wine glass – a simple device to stop flies crawling in! Someone added a slice of ham, an olive or a marinated pepper and – hey presto! – the *tapa* was born. An automatic companion to a small glass of wine, they range from slices of cheese or sausage to meatballs or snails. Every bar has its own speciality.

Another must is chocolate *con churros*, which are popular at breakfast or teatime. Cups of hot, thick drinking chocolate traditionally come with *churros*. Variously translated as doughnuts or fritters, these are light, crispy, deep-fried batter, shaped in Madrid-style teardrops, or in long, thick sticks, called *porras*. Dip them in sugar, or better still, dunk them in your hot chocolate.

Madrid hams (above) and wines from Chinchón and Valdepañas (below)

Wine

Spain is rich in vineyards, but in recent years there has been a renaissance in wine-making in the province of Madrid. Look for wines labelled D O Vinos de Madrid. Among the *blancos* (whites) try Albillo, Tapón de Oro and Viña Bayona. Refreshing *rosados* (rosés) are Tapón de Oro, Valfrío and Puerta del Sol, while reliable *tintos* (reds) include Valdeguerra and Tochuelo Tinto.

For those with a sweet tooth: hot chocolate and churros

🔲 41E4

The famous fountain on Plaza de la Cibeles

PLAZA DE LA CIBELES ✪

There are three spots dear to the hearts of *madrileños*: the Puerta de Alcalá arch; the statue of the bear and the *madroño* (madrona tree) in Puerto del Sol (► 64); and the Cibeles fountain in the roundabout that links the Paseo del Prado and the Paseo de Recoletos. Cybeles, the Greek goddess of fertility, sits in her chariot, which is drawn by two magnificent lions. The fountain itself was designed for Carlos III by Ventura Rodríguez in the 18th century, but these details are of little interest to Real Madrid football fans. They come here to celebrate their victories. Fans from rival Atlético de Madrid congregate at the next fountain to the south, with its statue of Neptune.

PLAZA MAYOR (► 25, TOP TEN)

🔲 29C2
✉ Calle de Alcalá 237
☎ 91 536 22 00 (stadium),
   91 725 18 57 (museum);
   www.las-ventas.com
🕐 Bullfights: Apr–Oct;
   Museum: 9:30–2:30.
   Closed Mon, Sat, public
   hols, on day of bullfight
   10–1
🍴 Plenty near by (€)
Ⓜ Las Ventas
♿ Stadium few; museum
   none
💶 Bullfights expensive;
   museum free

PLAZA DE TOROS DE LAS VENTAS ✪✪

Whether you are for or against bullfighting, Las Ventas is an astonishing building. Dating from 1929, this is the most prestigious arena in the world – a 22,000-seat cathedral of bullfighting. A classic example of Moorish-inspired architecture, with pink brick and decorative tilework, it towers above the Las Ventas Metro stop. In the spacious forecourt, lifesize statues make convenient meeting places for friends before a *corrida* (fight). Poised in mid-air to the left of the main entrance is '*El Yiyo*' (José Cubero), while the legendary Antonio Bienvenida is carried shoulder high by admirers (to the right of the main entrance). Off to one side, a *torero* doffs his cap to Dr Fleming, the inventor of penicillin, which has saved the lives of many bullfighters. Along a wall facing the southwest side of the stadium is a mural of nine lifesize bulls and their keepers.

Fights are usually at 7 in the evening, and are said to be the only events in Spain that start right on time. Crowds gather early looking for tickets and buying nuts and sweets from stalls. The most prestigious *corridas* are during the *feria* of San Isidro, the month-long festival in May, when some 30 take place.

On the north side of the arena is the **Museo Taurino**. This small museum is a Hall of Fame for bullfighting. It traces the development of the modern style and honours the legends of the ring, who are all known by their nicknames. Portraits and busts include stars of the 19th century: 'Cúchares' (Francisco Arjona), celebrated for his innovative movements, and the rivals 'Lagartijo' (Rafael Molina) and 'Frascuelo' (Salvador Sánchez). Although words such as 'artistic' and 'elegant' describe their skills, the litany of deaths from wounds and infections is sobering. The famous 'Manolete', for example, died after being gored on 28 August 1947. The white-and-gold costume he wore that day, plus his pink cape embroidered with roses and violets, is on display next to the basic blood transfusion machine that failed to save his life. Credit is also given to the supporting *picadores* and *banderilleros* and even famous bulls: the head of the bull that killed Manuel García Espartero (1865–94) is proudly displayed.

Madrid's Plaza de Toros de Las Ventas is the world's most prestigious bullring

Man and bull are commemorated in the Museo Taurino

40C3
Plenty near by (€)
Sol
Plaza Mayor (➤ 25)
Crammed on New Year's Eve

The Puerta del Sol marks the crossroads of the city

PUERTA DEL SOL

Streets radiate in all directions from this oblong plaza, literally the Gateway to the Sun and one of the focal points of Madrid. Dominating all he surveys is Carlos III (1759–88) astride a horse and usually with a pigeon perched on his royal head. The words on the plinth are a paean of praise to the king, who is regarded as 'the best mayor of Madrid'. He looks across at the handsome Casa de Correos, the post office from 1766–1847. To the right of the main entrance, a plaque honours the heroes of the *2 de mayo*, the rebellion on 2 May 1808 against the French army that had occupied the capital. Set in the pavement in front of the Casa de Correos, another plaque marks Kilometre 0, the *Origen de las Carreteras Radiales*. This is the point from which all distances to and from Madrid are measured. Other statues in this busy square include *La Mariblanca*, next to the station, and the emblem of Madrid – the famous *oso* (bear) standing on his hind legs and eating fruit from the *madroño* (madrona tree). Find it behind the Carlos III statue.

40B1

PUERTA DE TOLEDO

How are the mighty fallen! In 1808, when Frenchman Joseph Bonaparte was installed as king of Spain by his brother Napoleon, he gave orders for a triumphal arch to be erected at the Toledo gate. After Joseph was ousted by Fernando VII in 1814, work continued on the arch, but the triumph it celebrated was the Spanish defeat of the French! Another triumphal arch, the Puerta de Alcalá, is also lost in traffic, at the northwest corner of the Parque del Retiro. A symbol of Madrid, this is best appreciated at night, when it is tastefully floodlit.

EL RASTRO
(RASTRO FLEA MARKET)

Sunday would not be Sunday without a visit to the Rastro Flea Market. This sprawl of stalls attracts as many locals as visitors, even if they have no intention of buying anything. Start at the Plaza de Cascorro, with its statue of El Cascorro (Eloy Gonzalo), a 19th-century hero of the war in Cuba. The stalls here sell leather bags, weird crafts and perfumes of dubious origin. Once you reach the trees that shade Calle de la Ribera de Curtidores, the quality improves, with shops making solid furniture and wrought-iron weather vanes. Bars and pastry shops along the street are also open. In a courtyard, through an ancient arch, is the Galerías Piquer, a complex of 50 antiques shops selling everything from clocks to oriental furniture. Explore side streets such as Calle de San Cayetano, Calle de Rodas and Calle de Fray Ceferino González, lined with cages filled with budgerigars, pigeons and doves.

🔁 40C1
✉ Calle de Ribera de Curtidores
🕐 Sun, public hols AM
🍴 Plenty near by (€)
Ⓜ La Latina, Puerta de Toledo
🔄 Puerta de Toledo (➤ 64)

DID YOU KNOW?

The Casa de Correos clock is an integral part of Spain's New Year celebrations. As it strikes midnight, Spaniards all over the country watch television and eat *las uvas de la suerte* (lucky grapes), gulping down one grape per chime to ensure their good fortune in the new year.

Sunday fun at the Rastro flea market

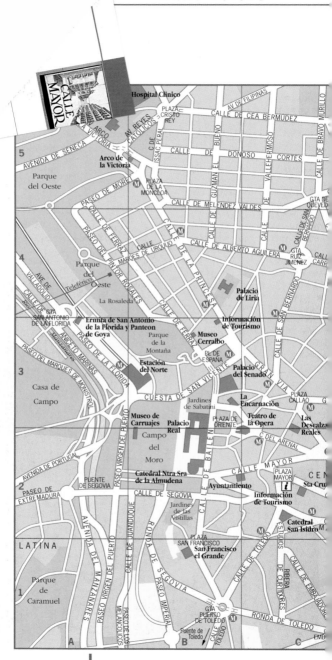

CALLE MAYOR

67

CALLE MAYOR

The Paseo del Prado

Distance
1.5km

Time
One day, including visits

Start point
Estación de Atocha
🚇 41E1
🚇 Estación de Atocha

End point
Plaza de la Cibeles
🚇 41E4
🚇 Banco de España

Tea
Hotel Ritz (€€)
✉ Plaza de la Lealtad 5
☎ 91 521 28 57

Start at the Atocha Railway Station.

The 19th-century station has been converted into an astonishing botanic garden; the high-speed trains leave from the hi-tech station annexe. Across the street is the Museo Nacional Centro de Arte Reina Sofía (➤ 19).

Walk north along the Paseo del Prado.

This is the southern end of a chain of boulevards passing several major attractions (➤ 59). Walk along the east side of the street, past the Real Jardín Botánico (➤ 70) and the Prado (➤ 26). On the left, in the Plaza de Cánovas del Castillo, is a fountain with a statue of Neptune. Beyond that is the Museo Thyssen-Bornemisza (➤ 22), the third of Madrid's spectacular art galleries.

The Puerta de Alcalá was built by Carlos III in the mid-18th century as a grand entrance to the city

Continue north on the Paseo del Prado.

Walk past the Hotel Ritz (Lealtad 5; ➤ 13, 102), and the railings on the Plaza de la Lealtad, which enclose an obelisk dedicated to the local heroes who died on 2 May 1808 in the revolt against the French. The next grand façade on the right (Lealtad 11) is the Bolsa, the Madrid Stock Exchange. Once past the Museo Naval (➤ 55), you reach the Plaza de la Cibeles (➤ 62), with its famous fountain. The grandiose building is the Palacio de Comunicaciones (➤ 57) , perhaps the most glamorous post office in the world. Off to the right, on the Calle de Alcalá, is the Puerta de Alcalá. This monumental arch, built by Carlos III, is considered the symbol of Madrid.

The Neptune fountain on the Plaza de Canovas del Castillo

⊞ 67F1
✉ Calle de Fuenterrabía 2
☎ 91 434 05 50
Mon–Fri 10–12:30
🍴 Plenty near by (€)
Ⓜ Atocha RENFE
♿ None
💵 Cheap
↔ Museo Nacional de
   Antropología (➤ 49)
❓ All visits in small guided
   groups

Above: *running repairs at
the Real Fábrica de
Tapices*

⊞ 41F2
✉ Plaza de Murillo 2
☎ 91 420 30 17
🕐 10–sunset
🍴 Plenty near by (€)
Ⓜ Atocha
♿ None
💵 Cheap
↔ Museo del Prado (➤ 26)
❓ Free guided tour (in
   Spanish) first Mon of
   month

Opposite: *ride the
Teleférico for great views
over the city*

REAL FÁBRICA DE TAPICES ✪✪

Not a museum, this factory hums with the sounds of men and women making and repairing carpets and tapestries. The methods have changed little, if at all, over the centuries since the van der Goten family were brought here from Flanders in the 18th century by Felipe V. The 200-year-old looms are still anchored by massive tree trunks to keep the tapestry taut, and woollen threads are still spun by hand, carefully mixed with silk to create some 3,000 subtly different shades.

Many of the tapestries are still based on cartoons by the famous Spanish painters of the day, including Goya (➤ 14). The time and effort required to complete a tapestry is astonishing: one square metre takes five months and costs over €9,000. Visitors tend to 'ooh' and 'aah' as they stare at workers who are using medieval skills in a medieval setting.

REAL JARDÍN BOTÁNICO ✪✪

On a hot summer day there is nowhere better to stroll or snooze on a bench than these royal botanic gardens. In celebration of its bicentenary (1981), the geometric gardens were renovated and remodelled; today there are three terraced areas to explore. Closest to the Paseo del Prado are 14 plots devoted to plants and herbs used for cooking, medicines and decoration. Some are indigenous to Spain and Portugal. In the late afternoon, enjoy the heady scent of the aromatics in plot 11. Dotted with fountains, the middle terrace is a living encyclopaedia of plants – from the oldest known to man to the most highly developed species – all arranged in the correct scientific order. Appropriately, a bust of Linnaeus, the Swedish botanist who invented this classification system for plants, overlooks the gardens. Like Kew Gardens in England, the Jardín Botánico is also a scientific institution, with a seed bank of plants from around the world as well as the Iberian Peninsula.

TELEFÉRICO

The most spectacular views of the Madrid skyline are from the Teleférico cable-car. Since 1969 it has glided from the Paseo del Pintor Rosales, just north of the Plaza de España, across to the scrubby parkland of the Casa de Campo. On board, a taped, but muffled, Spanish commentary points out landmarks as you swing across the newly planted gardens of the Parque del Oeste, the twin domes of the Ermita de San Antonio de la Florida (► 39) and the Río Manzanares. The 11-minute, 2.5km ride terminates in a modern block with a very ordinary cafetería and snack bar.

* 66A4
* Paseo del Pintor Rosales s/n
* 91 541 74 50
* Mon–Fri 11–3, 5–9:30; Sat, Sun, public hols 11–3, 5–10
* Restaurant/café (€)
* Argüelles
* None Moderate
* Ermita de San Antonio de la Florida (► 39)

TELEFÓNICA

One of the city's first skyscrapers, the Telefónica was designed by an American architect. Opened in 1929 as the headquarters of Spain's national telephone service, it symbolised the country's move into the modern era. A few years later, Franco's gunners used its 81m height as a gauge for shelling the Gran Vía during the Siege of Madrid. Take time to see the telephone company's collection of paintings and sculptures by Spanish artists such as Picasso, Chillida, Gris and Tapiès. Enter via the side door at Calle de Fuencarral 3.

* 41D4
* Gran Vía 28
* 91 522 66 45 (gallery)
* Tue–Fri 10–2, 5–8; Sat, Sun, public hols 10–2
* Plenty near by (€)
* Gran Vía
* Few
* Free
* Museo Chicote (► 54)

71

Calle de Alcalá

Distance
1.2km

Time
Half a day including visits

Start point
Banco de España
✚ 41E3
🚇 Banco de España

End point
Teatro Real
✚ 40B3
🚇 Opéra

Lunch/snack
Círculo de Bellas Artes (€)
✉ Calle del Marqués de
Casa Riera 2
☎ 91 531 85 03

Right: *one of Madrid's
most popular landmarks –
the bear and madroña
tree in the Puerta del Sol*

Below: *The refurbished
Teatro Real now has
one of the best
auditoriums in Europe*

*Start at the Banco de España Metro station and
walk west.*

The Calle de Alcalá runs east to the university town of
Alcalá de Henares. On the north side, where it converges
with the Gran Vía, is the 19th-century Iglesia de San José,
popular with South Americans who want to see where
early 19th-century revolutionary hero, Simón Bolívar was
married. Opposite is the elaborate 1926 Círculo de Bellas
Artes (No 42), an arts club with a café and outdoor terrace.
Anyone can pay a small fee for day membership, then
relax over coffee or a drink.

*Cross over and continue on the north side of the
Calle de Alcalá.*

At No 25 is the Iglesia de las Calatravas (➤ 45), a church
with an ornate façade. A few doors down is the Casino de
Madrid (No 15), a private gentleman's club, not a gambling
casino. No 13 is the Museo de la Real Academia de Bellas
Artes de San Fernando (➤ 51) and No 3 is the massive
Ministry of Finance, which was built as the Customs
House in the 18th century. The next square is the busy
Puerta del Sol (➤ 64).

*Carry on across the square to the Calle del
Arenal with its busy shops and restaurants.*

The first church on the left is San Ginés, with a painting by
Goya (open only for services). The walk ends at the Plaza
Isabel II, which is dominated by the Teatro Real.

In the Know

If you only have a short time to visit Madrid, or would like to get a real flavour of the city, here are some ideas:

10
Ways to Be a Local

Stop for a siesta – and enjoy the nightlife.
Cool off in the afternoon in a cinema on the Gran Vía (➤ 53).
Order a *horchata de chufa* – a traditional cold summer drink made from the *chufa* nut.
Play chess in the Parque del Retiro (➤ 24) on Sunday morning.
Go to a *zarzuela* (light opera) performance.
Drink hot chocolate with *churros* at dawn in the Chocolatería San Ginés (➤ 99).
Buy biscuits from the Convento de las Carboneras (➤ 38).
Watch the sunset by the Templo de Debod, below the Plaza de España.
Order a *cocido madrileño* (traditional stew) at La

Posada de la Villa (➤ 95).
Don't look like a tourist by wearing shorts and halter-tops; think smart casual.

10
Good Places to Have Lunch

Angel (€)
✉ Augusto Figueroa 35 ☎ 91 521 70 12. Near the Gran Vía but away from the tourists, this tiny, atmospheric bistro is ideal for an intimate lunch.

Brasserie de Lista (€)
✉ Calle de José Ortega y Gasset 6 ☎ 91 435 28 18. In Madrid's poshest shopping district. Sit outside under the parasols and count the carrier bags with designer labels passing by.

Café de Rosales (€)
✉ Paseo del Pintor de Rosales 36 ☎ 91 542 76 42. On a quiet *paseo* on the west side of town. Light snacks, good beers. Ideal

before or after a ride on the Teleférico (➤ 71).

A' Casiña (€–€€)
✉ Avenida del Angel s/n ☎ 91 526 34 25. Located in the Casa de Campo, so lunching here is like eating out in the country.

Casa Labra (€)
✉ Calle de Tuetuán 12 ☎ 91 513 00 81. Eat cod at the birthplace of the Spanish Socialist Party.

Casa Mingo (€)
✉ Glorieta de San Antonio de la Florida 2 ☎ 91 547 79 18. After seeing the Goya ceiling next door, everyone comes here for roast chicken, sausages and cider – plain, simple and cheap.

Gran Café Gijón (€)
✉ Paseo de Recoletos 21 ☎ 91 521 54 25. Order the menu of the day for a bargain lunch in plush art nouveau surroundings.

Enjoying a coffee at Bar Castellano on Paseo de la Castellana

Hotel Ritz (€€–€€€)
✉ Plaza de la Lealtad 5
☎ 91 521 28 57. The shady garden, scented by flowers, is a delightful spot for Sunday brunch. Expensive but worth it.

Museo Thyssen-Bornemisza (€)
✉ Paseo del Prado 8
☎ 91 429 27 32. Sit at the bar or at a table for modern food in a stylish setting, in the basement of the museum.

La Posada de la Villa (€)
✉ Calle de la Cava Baja 9
☎ 91 366 18 60. When exploring the old city, stop in this medieval tavern for a taste of some traditional, hearty dishes.

Great Views

From the glass elevators on the outside of the Museo Nacional Centro de Arte Reina Sofía (➤ 19)
From the top of Faro de Madrid, Avenida de los Reyes Católicos
☎ 91 722 04 00
From the swimming pool at the top of the Hotel Emperador, Gran Vía 53,
☎ 91 547 28 00
From a cable-car on the Teleférico (➤ 71)
From a café in the Jardines de las Vistillas

Private Art Galleries

Major companies have invested in modern art collections that are open to the public during office hours:
• Fundación Bancaja, Paseo de la Castellana 31
☎ 91 308 39 67
• Fundación Central Hispano, Calle del Marqués de Villamagna 3
☎ 91 575 14 30

The Faro de Madrid offers a 360° panoramic view

• Caixa Fundación, Calle Serrano 60
☎ 91 435 48 33
• Fundación Juan March, Calle de Castelló 77
☎ 91 435 42 40
• Fundación Telefónica, Fuencarral 3 (➤ 71)
☎ 91 522 66 45

Best *Terrazas*

Most open at 10PM and close in the early hours.
• **El Balcón de Rosales**, Paseo del Pintor Rosales/ Marqués de Urquijo
• **Bolero**, Paseo de la Castellana 33
• **El Espejo**, Paseo de los Recoletos 31
• **El Jardín de las Delicias**, Paseo de Cristino Martos 5
• **La Vieja Estación**, behind Atocha Railway Station

Things to Do on Sunday Morning

• Walk in the Retiro (➤ 24).
• See the stamp dealers in the Plaza Mayor (➤ 25).
• See the *Taller Abierto* (open studio) paintings in the Plaza del Conde de Barajas.
• Go to the Rastro Flea Market (➤ 65).
• Beat the crowds at the Museo Nacional Centro de Arte Reina Sofía and the Prado. Free all day Sun (➤ 19, 26).

Plaza Mayor

4 | Parque Santa María |

Campo de las Naciones

San Lorenzo ←

Aeropuerto (Barajas International) ✈

8 | Barajas |

8 | Mar de Cristal |

┌ Canillas

├ Esperanza

├ Arturo Soria

├ Avenida de la Paz

| Canillejas | **5**

┤ Torre Arias

┤ Suanzes

┤ Ciudad Lineal

Pío XII

Colombia

Concha Espina

Cruz del Rayo

Prosperidad

Alfonso XIII

Avenida de America

Cartagena

Parque de las Avenidas

Bario de la Concepción

┤ Pueblo Nuevo

┤ Ascao

┤ García Noblejas

┤ Simancas

┤ San Blas

Diego de León

| Ventas | **2**

El Carmen

Quintana

ez

oa

Lista

Manuel Becerra

quez

Goya

Príncipe de Vergara

O' Donnell

Ibíza

| Las Musas | **7**

ainz de Baranda

Estrella

Vinateros

Artilleros

Pavones

Conde de Casal

Valdebernardo

Vicálvaro

San Cipriano

Puerta de Arganda

Rivas Urbanicaciones

Rivas Vaciamadrid

La Poveda

cífico

uente de Vallecas

Nueva Numancia

Portazgo

Miguel Hernández

Villa de Vallecas

Buenos Aires

Alto del Arenal

Sierra de Guadalupe

| Congosto | **1**

| Arganda de Rey | **9**

Excursions from the City

Within a short drive or train ride from Madrid are some of the finest medieval towns in Europe. Toledo is not only the city of El Greco, but once boasted three distinct cultures; the pride of Alcalá de Henares was its great university; Segovia is dominated by a magnificent Roman aqueduct; and the jewel of Aranjuez is its royal palace. Since these towns are crowded with visitors during the holiday season, their rich blends of art and architecture, alleyways and hidden squares are best enjoyed in the evening or in the early morning. Consider staying overnight.

Also within the *comunidad* (autonomous community) of Madrid are the Sierra de Guadarrama to the north of the city. Dotted with small towns and villages, the mountains offer cool relief in summer, while in winter they are a popular destination for skiers.

> *This imperial gesture…still strode across the valley with massive grace, a hundred vistas framed by its soaring arches…stepping like a mammoth among the houses…*

LAURIE LEE
As I Walked out one Midsummer's Morning (1969)
(on the aqueduct at Segovia)

ALCALÁ DE HENARES ✪✪

In 1998, UNESCO recognised Alcalá de Henares as the first town designed and built exclusively as a university town. About 30km due east of Madrid, the Universidad Complutense was founded in 1498, and was soon one of Europe's great seats of learning. In the past 25 years, the area around the Plaza de Cervantes, the heart of the old town, has been successfully restored. What were *colegios* (or student halls of residence) have been converted into schools, hotels and restaurants, but the ornate Renaissance façade of the **Colegio Mayor de San Ildefonso** (University of Alcalá de Henares) gives some idea of the original grandeur of the university headquarters. This administered 40 colleges and 10,000 students. Inside were three *patios* or courtyards. The third, El Trilingüe (1557), was where students from the schools of Hebrew, Greek and Latin would meet to chat in three languages. The Paraninfo (Great Hall) is still used for solemn university ceremonies, while the 15th-century chapel of San Ildefonso holds a richly-sculpted marble memorial to the hugely influential Catholic leader, Cardinal Cisneros, the founder of the university.

Alcalá de Henares was also the birthplace of Miguel de Cervantes Saavedra (1547–1616), author of the international favourite, *El Quijote* (or *Don Quixote*). At No 48 on the attractive Calle Mayor main street is the **Casa Natal de Cervantes**. This is a reproduction of the writer's alleged birthplace, with an interior *patio* typical of the 16th century, and appropriate furniture for the era. Be sure to take home the local delicacy: *almendras garrapiñadas* (caramel covered almonds).

🚩 81E3

🚆 Cervantes Train: weekends May–Jun, leaves Atocha Madrid 11AM, departs Alcalá 6:35PM

ℹ️ Callejón Santa María 2
☎ 91 889 26 94
🕐 Jul–Aug, 10–2, 5–7; Sep–Jun 10–2, 4–6:30

Colegio Mayor de San Ildefonso
✉️ Plaza de San Diego
☎ 91 885 40 00
🕐 Mon–Fri guided tours 11:30, 12:30, 1:30, 5, 6, Sat, Sun 11, 11:45, 12:30,1:15, 3:45, 6:30, 7:15, 8
🖐 Cheap

Casa Natal de Cervantes
✉️ Calle Mayor 48
☎ 91 889 96 54
🕐 Mon–Fri 10:15–2, 4–6:45, Sat, Sun 10:15–1:45, 4–6:30
🖐 Free

The university at Alcalá de Henares was reborn in the 1970s

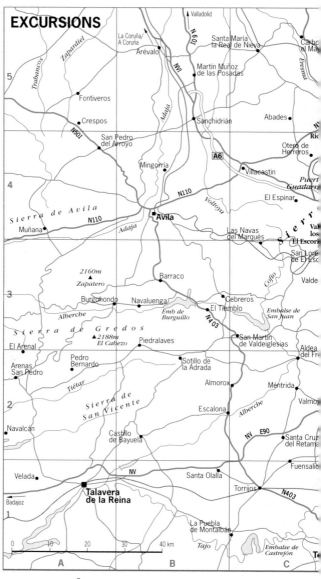

EXCURSIONS

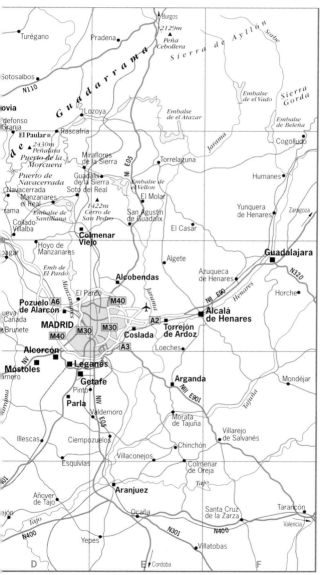

🔳 81E1

🚆 *Tren de la Fresa*, Atocha,
Madrid weekends 10AM
Apr–Oct (not Aug)
☎ 91 328 90 20

🍴 Plenty near by (€)

ℹ Plaza de San Antonio 9
☎ 91 891 04 27
🕐 Tue–Sun 10–2, 4–6
(summer); 10–1, 3–5
(winter)

❓ 35-min tour on tourist
trolley. Hourly from
tourist office, from 10AM
(not Mon, public hols)
☎ 925 14 22 74

**Palacio Real, Casa del
Labrador**
☎ 91 891 07 40
🕐 Tue–Sun 10–6:15
(summer); 10–5:15
(winter)
💶 Cheap, Wed free EU
citizens

*The Real Capilla de San
Antonio (Royal Chapel),
Aranjuez*

ARANJUEZ ⭐⭐⭐

Thanks to the haunting theme of the *Concierto de Aranjuez* by Joaquín Rodrigo, music-lovers around the world know the name of this town. Just 50km south of Madrid, Aranjuez became a royal retreat 300 years ago. Today it is a popular destination for *madrileños*, who come for a day out, particularly in early summer when the asparagus and *fresones* (large local strawberries) are in season. They stroll along tree-lined boulevards and through the gardens, take a boat ride on the Río Tajo (River Tagus) and tour the **Palacio Real**. This enormous baroque palace was built in the early 18th century for Felipe V. Although the façade and the interior remain much as they were, two wings were added later. Inside are paintings and frescoes and, best of all, the Sala de las Porcelanas. The porcelain tiles, made in Madrid, portray scenes from Chinese life, as well as children's games.

Heading east from the palace, follow the Calle de la Reina to the 150ha Jardín del Principe and, further along, the **Casa del Labrador**. Whimsically named the Worker's Cottage, it is opulently decorated and full of treasures, such as the Gabinete de Platino, with idazzling inlays of platinum, gold and bronze. Aranjuez is at its loveliest in March and April when the gardens are in bloom, but is most fun in May during the festivities for San Fernando (30 May) and in September, during the Fiestas del Motín. On weekends between April and October take the *Tren de la Fresa* (Strawberry Train) with its wooden carriages, steam engine and costumed hostesses distributing strawberries.

Old Towns South of Madrid

This route south includes three historic towns: one ancient, one royal and one a fortress.

Leave Madrid on the M-30/E-901, then take the A-3 for Chinchón. Before the main exit to Arganda, take the turning for Chinchón, the M-311. Take the left turn for Morata de Tajuña, with its view over the valley. Once on flat ground, you pass Anís de Chinchón, the distillery of the popular aniseed-flavoured drink. Then it's up to the opposite ridge, and down into the next valley, where Chinchón stands high on a hillside.

Distance
200km

Time
9 hours with stops, 5 hours without stops

Start/end point
Madrid
✛ 81E3

Lunch
La Perdiz (€–€€)
✉ Calle de los Reyes Católicos 7, Toledo
☎ 925 21 46 58

Head for the Plaza Mayor, a perfect film set for a costume drama in medieval Spain. Surrounded by rows of balconied houses, it is a ready-made arena, where bullfights and theatrical performances are still held. Have lunch at one of the many restaurants with tables outdoors. A former convent has been converted into a stylish *parador*. Parking is difficult in town, so leave the car on the outskirts and walk into the centre.

From Chinchón, take the M-305 for Aranjuez.

Chinchón retains medieval memories

Villaconejos, known for its melons, is a typical blend of old and new, the attractive and bland. Carry on to the royal town of Aranjuez (➤ 82).

From Aranjuez, take the N-400 for Ocaña and Toledo.

You can see Toledo's castle from afar, standing guard over the plain below. Park in one of the car parks at the foot of the hill and explore this walled city on foot (➤ 88).

Return to Madrid on the N-401 motorway.

✚	80C3
☎	92 890 15 44
🕐	Tue–Sun 10–7 (summer); 10–6 (winter)
🍴	Plenty near by (€)
♿	Few
🎫	Moderate
❓	Regular foreign language guided tours from Calle Floridablanca 10

Valle de los Caídos

✚	80C4
☎	91 890 56 11
🕐	Tue–Sun 9:30–7 (summer); 10–6 (winter)
♿	Few
🎫	Moderate

Above: *the vast and rather forbidding façade of El Escorial monastery*

✚ 81D4

EL ESCORIAL ✪✪✪

The first impression of the Real Monasterio de San Lorenzo de El Escorial is always its vast size. Some 50km northwest of Madrid, this combination of monastery, palace and royal mausoleum was built to celebrate victory against the French in the battle of St Quentin in 1557. Six years later, Felipe II set out to flaunt Spain's roles as rulers of the world and as the bulwark of Roman Catholicism against the forces of the Reformation. It took only 21 years to complete and has 1,200 doors, 2,600 windows and some 24km of corridors. The result must have impressed both the king's subjects and his European rivals.

The interior is surprisingly austere, reflecting Felipe II's taste. Highlights include the Nuevos Museos (New Museum of Art), with major works by Titian, Tintoretto, Veronese, Rubens and van Dyck. Among several fine paintings by El Greco are *The Martyrdom of St Maurice* (one of his finest, though Felipe II did not like it) and *The Dream of Felipe II*, portraying the ascetic king at prayer in paradise. The heart of El Escorial is the vast basilica, which is reminiscent of St Peter's in Rome, while the library (one of Felipe II's pet projects) holds an important collection of 15th- and 16th-century books. With its lavish baroque decoration, the pantheon is the burial place of the Spanish royal family. Carlos I was the first to be buried there. Expect crowds at weekends.

Marked by a 150m high cross, the **Valle de los Caídos** (Valley of the Fallen), 9km north, is a monument to General Franco and the Falangists (the Spanish Fascists).

MANZANARES EL REAL ✪

In summer, *madrileños* head for the cooler heights of the Sierra de Guadarrama and the town of Manzanares El Real, 47km north of the capital. Legend has it that Felipe II considered establishing El Escorial (➤ above) here.

Left: *the grandiose library at El Escorial holds 40,000 books, plus precious manuscripts and codices*

Certainly the 15th-century castle, with its backdrop of the Sierra de Pedriza, is dramatic. Built for the dukes of Infantado, the fortress retains Moorish features such as honeycomb cornices. Below, quiet gardens border the banks of the Río Manzanares.

Above: *flag flying on one of the turrets of Manzanares castle*

EL PARDO ✪

Like the Valle de los Caídos (➤ 84), El Pardo has uncomfortable associations with the recent past, as the Palacio del Pardo was General Franco's main residence for some 35 years. However, before that, the village was a royal favourite for centuries. Felipe II and Carlos III came to hunt, and added to the comforts of the elegant 16th-century palace, which is now used to entertain foreign heads of state. (The present royal family lives just 5km away at the Zarzuela Palace).

Only 8km northwest of Madrid, this is another retreat for *madrileños*, who relax at the exclusive country clubs. Although part of the palace is open, the public rarely comes in numbers. However, the 200 Flemish and Spanish tapestries, as well as paintings by Spanish masters, are of interest, especially when combined with lunch at a restaurant on the Avenida de la Guardia, where game is a speciality.

➕ 81D3
✉ Paseo del Pardo
☎ 91 376 00 56
🕐 Mon–Sat 10:30–6, Sun, public hols 9:25–1:40 (summer); 10:30–5, Sun, public hols 9:55–1:40 (winter). Closed occasionally for official functions
🍴 Plenty near by (€)
♿ Cheap

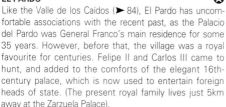

Segovia's magnificent Roman aqueduct still looms over the city

🕂 81D5

🍴 Plenty (€)

🏛 Plaza del Azoguejo
   ☎ 921 46 29 06
   🕐 10–8; Plaza Mayor 10
   ☎ 921 46 03 34
   🕐 10–2, 5–8

❓ Free guided tours of
   Segovia start here,
   Jul–Sep 10, 11, 12 (inner
   city), 4:30 (outer city)

❓ 40-minute tour on tourist
   trolley. Mon–Thu, Sun
   runs on the hour 11–1,
   4–6, Fri, Sat 11–1, 4–11
   ☎ 925 14 22 74

El Alcázar

✉ Plaza de la Reina Victoria
   Eugenia
   ☎ 921 46 07 59
   🕐 10–7 (summer); 10–6
   (winter)
   ♿ Few
   ✋ Cheap

SEGOVIA ⭐⭐⭐

The old city of Segovia is surprisingly intact and unspoiled by 20th-century buildings. Standing between the Río Eresma and the Arroyo Clamores, with the Sierra de Guadarrama as a backdrop, the city's strategic importance explains its long history.

Segovia is best known for its Roman aqueduct. You can't miss the two tiers of 163 arches built of precisely cut granite, without mortar. Standing 29m above the ground at its highest point, it stretches for 813m; the water that once flowed along the channel started its journey some 15km away. This is an awesome piece of civil engineering; by comparison, the brick-and-mortar city wall looks positively messy.

Pick up a map at the tourist information office on Plaza del Azoguejo and head off to explore the old streets. Follow Calle de Cervantes, where the façade of the Casa de los Picos looks like a studded shield. This delightful street of half-timbered houses with wrought-iron balconies changes name as it winds its way uphill; perhaps that is why locals just call it the Calle Real. At the top are the Plaza Mayor and the 16th-century cathedral. Further along the Calle Real is El Alcázar. Looking like Sleeping Beauty's castle, complete with turrets and towers, it stands on top of sheer cliffs, with commanding views across the plain below. Late on Friday and Saturday nights, the city's ancient monuments are illuminated. No visit is complete without sampling the slow-cooked lamb or *cochinillo* (suckling pig), so tender that only a fork is needed.

Segovia and the Mountains

This route heads northwest past El Escorial and Segovia, before heading for La Granja and a spectacular mountain pass.

Leave Madrid on the A-6; take the exit for El Escorial. This road becomes the M-505.

The massive palace of El Escorial (➤ 84) dominates the old town, with its attractive squares and narrow streets.

From El Escorial, route M-600 to Guadarrama passes the entrance to the Valle de los Caídos (➤ 84) and heads into the tunnel beneath the Puerto de Guadarrama, 1,611m above sea level. Take the N-603 for Segovia.

Don't be put off by the modern outskirts of Segovia, the old heart of the city has an undeniable charm (➤ 86) and is an excellent place to stop for lunch, with a walk before or afterwards.

From Segovia, the CL-601, signposted Madrid and La Granja, leads up into the hills.

Distance
200km

Time
9 hours with stops, 5 hours without stops

Start/end point
Madrid
✚ 81D3

Lunch
Cava Duque (€–€€)
✉ Calle de Cervantes 12, Segovia
☎ 921 46 24 87

Real Fábrica de Cristales
✉ Paseo del Pocillo 1, La Granja de San Ildefonso, Segovia
☎ 921 47 17 12
🕐 Tue–Sat 10–6, Sun 10–3
💷 Cheap

The Riofrío Palace at La Granja de San Ildefonso

The main attraction in La Granja de San Ildefonso is Felipe V's romantic 18th-century palace, a mini-Versailles. Near by is the Riofrío Palace, built by Felipe's widow, and the **Real Fábrica de Cristales**. In the 18th century, this factory made spectacular chandeliers and mirrors for royal palaces. Today, the craft has been revived in the factory, school and museum.

From La Granja, the CL-601 climbs through peaceful woods, past signs proclaiming ever-increasing altitudes. Admire the view at Puerto de la Navacerrada, a ski resort right at the tree line (1880m). Return to Madrid via the M-601, through Navacerrada, and the N-6.

Above: *a souvenir of Toledo*
Right: *the Puerta de los Leones, on the south side of Toledo Cathedral*

🕂 80C1
ℹ️ Puerta de Bisagra s/n
☎ 925 22 08 43
🕐 Mon–Fri 9–6, Sat 9–7, Sun, public hols 9–3
🍴 Plenty (€–€€)
❓ 50-minute tour through old town on tourist trolley. Starts Plaza de Zocodover
☎ 925 25 22 74
🕐 From 11AM; also at night, weekends

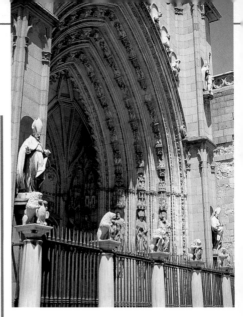

TOLEDO ✪✪✪

Don't miss Toledo. Few cities have such a rich tapestry of art, religion and history. Ironically, a 16th-century painter from Crete is most closely associated with this city, set high on a bluff above the Río Tajo (River Tagus). El Greco (The Greek) painted his greatest works here, including a menacing landscape of the city dominated by its cathedral and fortress. Both still punctuate the skyline of this medieval city, with its steep streets and twisting alleyways.

Toledo is often called the 'city of the three cultures', reflecting the harmony and prosperity enjoyed by Christians, Jews and Muslims during the Middle Ages. The Islamic heritage is recalled in the Moorish architecture, with characteristic keyhole arches and forbidding doors hiding beautiful courtyards. In the Judería (the Jewish quarter), two of the original eight synagogues survive. These were renovated in 1992, along with many houses, five centuries after the expulsion of all Jews from Spain. The cathedral, started in 1226, is one of Spain's largest and after the royal court moved to Madrid in 1560, Toledo remained the country's religious capital.

A mini-lesson in Spanish history, with Roman, Visigoth and Moorish connections, this ancient stronghold became the capital of Castile in 1085. It thrived as a centre of learning, commerce and religious tolerance. Toledo swords and armour were famous throughout Europe. Although there are more than enough museums and churches to admire, the best way to appreciate Toledo is to be there at night after the tourists have left.

Toledo

This atmospheric walk takes in all the important sights. Toledo has steep hills and cobblestone streets, so wear comfortable shoes.

Start at the Plaza de Zocodover.

Through the large Moorish archway under the clock steps lead to the **Museo de Santa Cruz**, a fine museum known for its El Greco paintings. Up the hill on Cuesta Carlos V is the Alcázar fortress.

From the plaza, follow Calle de Comercio. Turn left to the front of the Cathedral.

Toledo's crowning glory, the Alcázar fortress

This enormous Gothic structure is a treasure chest of religious art. The sacristy is hung with works by El Greco, van Dyck and Goya.

Cross the square, follow the alley to the right of the town hall; it narrows into a passageway and you step through a doorway into a tiny square. Turn right on to Calle de El Salvador. Go uphill to Calle de Santo Tomé. Turn left on San Juan de Dios for the Iglesia de Santo Tomé.

Underneath its Moorish tower, the 14th-century church houses El Greco's huge painting, *The Burial of the Count of Orgaz*. Across the square, the **Casa-Museo de El Greco** is dedicated to the famous painter.

From here, Calle de San Juan de Dios leads into the Jewish quarter. Continue to the Sinagoga del Tránsito.

With Moorish and Gothic details, this 14th-century synagogue reflects the three cultures of Toledo; the Sephardic Museum explains the traditions of Spanish Jews.

From here, return to the Plaza de Zocodover or wander through more ancient alleyways.

Distance
1km, hilly

Time
1 hour without stops, 5 hours with stops

Start
Plaza de Zocodover

End
Sinagoga del Tránsito

Lunch
Casa Aurelio (€–€€)
✉ Sinagoga 6
☎ 925 22 20 97

Museo de Santa Cruz
✉ Calle de Cervantes 3
☎ 925 22 10 36
🕐 10–6:30, Sun 10–2
✋ Cheap

Casa-Museo de El Greco
✉ Calle de Samuel Leví 3
☎ 925 22 40 46
🕐 Tue–Sat 10–2, 4–6, Sun 10–2
✋ Cheap

Guadarrama Mountains

Lovely in spring and autumn, this scenic drive north through the green Guadarrama Mountains is also a cool escape from Madrid in the height of summer.

Leave Madrid on the A-6; turn on to the M-608 at Collado Villalba. Continue to Manzanares el Real.

The 15th-century castle at Manzanares el Real (➤ 85) stands proudly, its battlements, watchtowers and fortifications looking as if they have sprouted from the rock.

The towers and glory of Manzanares el Real, now beautifully restored

Continue on the M-608, turn left on the M-611 for Miraflores de la Sierra.

The road climbs through ranches where massive fighting bulls are bred for the *corrida* (fight). The quiet is broken only by birdsong. In spring and early summer there are wild flowers. On the side of a steep hill, Miraflores is a perfect stop for lunch, with fine views.

Continue on the M-611.

At the pass of Puerto de la Morchera (1,786m), enjoy even more spectacular views across to snowy peaks – even in June. In summer, you pass bushes of wild roses; in autumn, the oaks turn golden brown. The narrow road twists and turns past *refugios*, stone huts for walkers. Just outside Rascafría is a 14th-century monastery; part of it is now a hotel.

At the village of Rascafría, turn right on to the M-604 and continue to Lozoya.

The small village of Lozoya is another good place to stop and stretch your legs before having lunch or a snack.

Follow signs for the N-1 (the E-05), the motorway south to Madrid.

Distance
175km

Time
4 hours, mountain roads

Start/end
Madrid
 81D3

Lunch
Hotel Santa María del Paular
(€€)
✉ N-604, Rascafría
☎ 91 869 10 11

Where To...

Above: *a picture is worth a thousand words*
Right: *kids just wanna have fun in the park*

Madrid

Prices

Madrileños say that there is a bank, a pharmacy, a church and a bar on every block. Certainly food and drink are never more than a minute away. Restaurant prices are based on a three-course meal for one, without drinks or service.

€   = under €15
€€   = €15–30
€€€ = over €30

Set Meals

Most restaurants offer a lunchtime *menú del día* (fixed price meal) of around €8 which usually includes an appetizer, main course, dessert and wine or water. This offers great value but limited choice. The price includes VAT but not service; leave 5–10 percent depending on the quality of service. If you eat à la carte, it will cost more, but you can then sample the specialities.

Madrid has well over 17,000 places to eat, but there are times when visitors, especially with children, want somewhere quick, easy and international. The city has several chains of simple but good restaurants that serve meals and snacks with a Spanish accent at low prices. These are open throughout the day, from early in the morning until late into the night.

Angel (€)

Once nicknamed El Comunista for its anti-Franco clientele, this is a well-priced, fun, neighbourhood eatery across from the Mercado de San Antón. At the back are tiny tables with red tablecloths.

✉ **Augusto Figueroa 35**
☎ **91 521 70 12** 🕐 Lunch, dinner. Closed Sun, public hols 🚇 **Chueca**

El Asador de Aranda (€€)

This restaurant serves the regional speciality of Castile: lamb roasted slowly in a wood-fired oven. Order the local red wines from the province of Madrid.

✉ **Calle Preciados 44** ☎ **91 547 21 56** 🕐 Lunch, dinner. Closed Mon dinner 🚇 **Sol**

La Barraca (€€)

This is the place for authentic *paella* and other rice-based specialities from the Valencian region. Best accompanied by the white wines from Valencia.

✉ **Calle de la Reina 29**
☎ **91 532 71 54** 🕐 Lunch, dinner 🚇 **Banco de España**

La Bola (€€)

Behind the Plaza del Oriente, this is the sort of place

where locals bring their out-of-town friends for authentic *cocido madrileño* (Madrid stew). Open since 1870; no credit cards.

✉ **Calle de la Bola 5**
☎ **91 547 69 30** 🕐 Lunch, dinner. Closed Sun dinner 🚇 **Santo Domingo**

El Botín (➤ 33)

Brasserie de Lista (€–€€)

In the expensive Serrano shopping area, this stylish yet informal restaurant serves international dishes, with grilled meat a speciality. The equally stylish Taberna de Lista is at No 89.

✉ **Calle de José Ortega y Gasset 6** ☎ **91 435 28 18** 🕐 Lunch, dinner. Closed Sat lunch, Sun 🚇 **Núñez de Balboa**

El Buey (€€€)

Its name means ox, and beef is the speciality, with prime cuts, sold Spanish-style by weight. There are alternative fish dishes. Booking is essential.

✉ **Plaza de la Marina Española 1** ☎ **91 541 30 41** 🕐 Lunch, dinner. Closed Sun dinner 🚇 **Opera, Santo Domingo**

Café & Té (€)

With colourful walls and straw hats, the theme is Colombian. There are some eight branches in this growing chain. As well as coffee and tea, they sell milk shakes, *frappés* (cold iced drinks) and snacks.

Café de la Opera (€€)

Right by the Teatro Real opera house. The waiters and waitresses are opera students, who serve and sing opera and *zarzuela* (light opera). Well-prepared international dishes.

✉ **Calle de Arrieta 6**
☎ 91 542 63 82 🕐 **Dinner only** Ⓜ Opera

Casa Gallega (€€)
Galician restaurants specialize in seafood. Try *sopa de mariscos* (fish soup) or *cogote de merluza* (hake baked in the oven). Also at Plaza de San Miguel, near the market.

✉ **Calle de Bordadores 11**
☎ 91 541 90 55 🕐 **Lunch, dinner** Ⓜ Sol

Casa Lucio (€€) ✗
Popular with the royal family, foreign politicians and film stars. A fashionable but affordable restaurant on Madrid's restaurant row that is known for Castilian dishes such as stews and roasts. Booking essential.

✉ **Calle de la Cava Baja 35**
☎ 91 365 32 52 🕐 **Lunch, dinner. Sat dinner only. Closed Aug** Ⓜ La Latina

A'Casiña (€€)
On a warm day this is an ideal spot for lunch outdoors on the terrace, hidden by greenery from the road through the Casa del Campo. Order Galician specialities, especially seafood. Reservations essential.

✉ **Avenida del Angel, Casa de Campo** ☎ 91 526 34 25
🕐 **Lunch, dinner. Closed Sun dinner** Ⓜ El Lago

El Cenador del Prado (€€–€€€)
When you want to try contemporary Spanish cuisine, this is one of the best. Near the Plaza Santa Ana. To enjoy the best of the Heranz brothers, try the *menú de degustación*

(special tasting menu).

✉ **Calle del Prado 4**
☎ 91 429 15 61 🕐 **Lunch, dinner. Closed Sat lunch, Sun**
Ⓜ Antón Martín, Sevilla

La Chata (€€)
Reputed to be a favourite among bullfighters, the menu features roast suckling pig, lamb and langoustines with sherry sauce or wild mushrooms. Good *tapas* and wines by the glass.

✉ **Cava de la Baja 24**
☎ 91 366 14 58 🕐 **Lunch, dinner. Closed Tue, Wed lunch**
Ⓜ La Latina

Chez Pomme (€)
The vegetarian cooking here is imaginative: sweet red pepper pâté, broccoli crêpe, baked aubergines and béchamel sauce. Six freshly squeezed juices. No credit cards.

✉ **Calle de Pelayo 4**
☎ 91 532 16 46 🕐 **Lunch, dinner. Closed Sun** Ⓜ Chueca

Las Cuevas de Luis Candelas (€€–€€€)
Just off the Plaza Mayor, this traditional tavern offers Castilian dishes, especially roast lamb and pork. Touristy but fun, with plenty of locals, especially for Sunday lunch.

✉ **Calle de los Cuchilleros 1**
☎ 91 366 54 28 🕐 **Lunch, dinner** Ⓜ Sol

Dantxari (€€–€€€)
This Basque tavern has spicy cod, lamb with garlic and wild mushrooms. Wide-ranging Spanish wine list, cheerful service.

✉ **Ventura Rodriguez 8**
☎ 91 542 35 24 🕐 **Lunch, dinner. Closed Sun dinner**
Ⓜ Plaza España

Opening Times
The Spanish like to eat late. Restaurants tend to serve lunch from 1–3 and dinner from 9–12AM. Cafés are open most of the day and often into the early hours of the morning. *Tapas* bars open from 11–3 and 5 or 6 until late. If you want to sit down to a proper meal in the evening, it is worth phoning ahead to check the opening time and to book a table. During the summer months, particularly August, some establishments close.

Sweets for my Sweet

The *madrileños* love their traditional sweet cakes. During the festival of San Isidro, look out for *rosquillas*, like a ring-shaped doughnut, which comes in several flavours. *Tontas* (stupid) are plain but *listas* (clever) are dipped in sugar and lemon; *Santa Clara* and *Tía Javiera* are soaked in brandy. *Bartolillos* are three-cornered pies. Traditionally eaten during Holy Week, *torrijas* are crunchy, like French toast, but can be enjoyed year-round with a glass of sweet wine at El Rey de los Vinos. At Halloween, pastry shops sell *huesos de santos* (saints' bones) and *buñuelos* (like a doughnut).

La Gastroteca de Stéphane y Arturo (€€€)

Madrid's most avant-garde restaurant. Stéphane Guérin's menu has seven skate dishes, *foie gras* with honey, vinegar and fig compote, and the intriguingly-named 'pornological' hamburger made from *magret* of duck.

✉ Plaza de Chueca 8
☎ 91 532 25 64 🍴 Lunch, dinner. Closed Sat lunch, Sun, public hols, Aug 🚇 Chueca

Los Girasoles (€–€€)

Stylish and trendy, with yellow walls and blue tablecloths. Modern Spanish cooking as well as classic dishes such as *paella* (Wed) and *cocido* (Thu). Excellent range of regional wines.

✉ Calle de la Hortaleza 106
☎ 91 308 44 94 🍴 Lunch, dinner. Closed Sat lunch, Sun 🚇 Alonso Martínez

Horcher (€€€)

Step back in time to old-fashioned luxury. Wild duck, venison and boar are the specialities in this German-influenced traditional businessmen's haunt.

✉ Alfonso XIII 6
☎ 91 522 07 31 🍴 Lunch, dinner. Closed Sat lunch, Sun 🚇 Retiro

Lhardy (€€€)

In 1839, the author of *Carmen* persuaded Emile Lhardy to open a French restaurant in Madrid and it is still going strong. Beautiful, historic and expensive: pheasant with grapes, sole in champagne sauce.

✉ Carrera de San Jerónimo 8
☎ 91 521 33 85 🍴 Lunch, dinner. Closed Sun, public hols dinner 🚇 Sevilla, Sol

Malacatín (€–€€)

Despite its echoes of the Franco era, this is still a friendly little spot near the Rastro Flea Market. Another favourite with locals who order *cocido* (Madrid stew).

✉ Calle de la Ruda 5 ☎ 91 365 52 41 🍴 Lunch, dinner. Closed Sat dinner, Sun, public hols, Jul, Aug 🚇 La Latina

Museo del Jamón (€–€€)

This 30-year-old family enterprise has five downtown branches, hung with thousands of dried Serrano hams. Expect light meals, pastries and coffee, as well as fresh bread to take away.

La Panera (€€)

A small corner of Asturias, featuring hearty dishes from northern Spain: *fabada* (pork and beans), *fabes con almejas* (beans and mussels). Order cider to drink. Plain décor.

✉ Calle del Arenal 19
☎ 91 542 92 20 🍴 1–4, 8–12 🚇 Opera, Sol

Pans & Company (€)

This chain sells Spanish-style fast food, as well as hot, wholemeal and grilled sandwiches, salads, ice-creams and cold drinks.

Paradís Madrid (€€€)

The original Paradís opened in Barcelona in 1954; the three branches in Madrid serve stylish, modern Catalan cooking, with notably good seafood. There is even a menu of olive oils.

✉ Calle Marqués de Cubas 14
☎ 91 429 73 03 🍴 Lunch, dinner. Closed Sat lunch, Sun, public hols, Aug 🚇 Banco de España

La Posada de la Villa (€€–€€€)

An inn since 1642, but now a restaurant famous for its whole roasted milk-fed lamb, baked in a special stone oven just inside the entrance. Close to the Plaza Mayor.

✉ **Calle de la Cava Baja 9**
☎ **91 366 18 60** 🕐 **Lunch, dinner. Closed Sun dinner, Aug**
🚇 **La Latina**

Taberna del Sarmiento (€€)

Since 1998, chef Gabi Gomez has given traditional dishes a modern twist. Try beetroot *gazpacho*, home-made *foie gras*, above-average desserts. Notably good wines by the glass. Reservation recommended.

✉ **Calle de la Hortaleza 28**
☎ **91 531 15 71** 🕐 **Lunch, dinner. Closed Sun**
🚇 **Chueca, Alonso Martínez**

La Trainera (€€–€€€)

A plain restaurant in the expensive Serrano district, this is one of the best places for fish in Madrid. Try oysters, crabs, *gambas* (prawns), *sopa de mariscos* (fish soup).

✉ **Calle Lagasca 60** ☎ **91 576 80 35** 🕐 **Lunch, dinner. Closed Sun, Aug** 🚇 **Serrano**

La Trucha (€–€€)

Specialising in Andalucian dishes in general and trout in particular, this is the sister restaurant of the *tapas* bar of the same name. Both are just off the Plaza de Santa Ana.

✉ **Calle de Núñez de Arce 6**
☎ **91 532 08 82** 🕐 **Lunch, dinner. Closed Sun, Mon**
🚇 **Sol**

La Vaca Argentina (€–€€€)

Homesick Argentinians come here for big steaks, cooked to perfection. Like its sister restaurants, this branch near the Teatro Real opera house is informal and ranch-style.

✉ **Calle de los Caños del Peral 2** ☎ **91 541 33 18**
🕐 **Lunch, dinner** 🚇 **Opera**

VIPS (€)

A combination shop and restaurant. Menus include familiar dishes, surroundings are cafeteria-style, and you can buy useful things such as newspapers, film, toiletries and maps.

Viridiana (€€€)

Near the three famous art museums, this is imaginative modern Spanish cooking at its best, thanks to chef Abraham Garcia. Perhaps the best wine list in Spain.

✉ **Calle de Juan de Mena 14**
☎ **91 531 52 22** 🕐 **Lunch, dinner. Closed Sun, public hols, Aug**
🚇 **Banco de España, Retiro**

Viuda de Vacas (€€)

Home-style Castilian cooking, from oxtail to tripe, is the speciality of this atmospheric oak-beamed restaurant with its twisting staircase, tiles and wood oven.

✉ **Calle de la Cava Alta 23**
☎ **91 366 58 47** 🕐 **Lunch, dinner. Closed Sun dinner, Thu, public hols, Aug** 🚇 **La Latina**

Zalacaín (€€€)

This has a reputation as Madrid's top restaurant, with an international menu and Basque specialities. Advance booking essential.

✉ **Calle de Alvarez de Baena 4** ☎ **91 561 10 79** 🕐 **Lunch, dinner. Closed Sat lunch, Aug, Easter** 🚇 **Gregorio Marañón**

Madrid Specialities

Traditional restaurants in the city have wood-fired ovens where whole milk-fed lamb and suckling pig are slowly and gently roasted. In autumn and winter, look for game, *rabo de toro* (oxtail stew) and *cocido madrileño* (Madrid stew), cooked in a *puchero* (clay pot) on a wood fire.

Tapas Bars

Drinks

Madrid has a dry climate and in summer is very hot, but wherever you are, you are never far from a cold drink. Here are some useful words when you need to slake your thirst.

agua mineral: mineral water
caña: small glass of beer
clara: beer and lemonade (shandy)
cubata: rum and coke
fino: dry sherry
de grifo: draught (beer, vermouth)
tubo: large beer
vermú: vermouth
vino blanco: white wine
vino tinto: red wine

Alkalde (€)

A *tapas* bar with a difference: the Basque name is a clue to the Basque-style *tapas*, which include *tortilla* with red peppers and seafood. Handy for shopping sprees in the upmarket Salamanca district.

📧 **Calle de Jorge Juan 10**
☎ **91 576 33 59** 🕔 **Lunch, dinner. Closed Jul, Aug**
🚇 **Serrano**

El Almendro 13 (€)

This bar specialises in hearty Andalucian cooking, so ask for a *manzanilla* from Sanlúcar with your *tapas*. If you order a *ración* (large portion), a bell is rung when it is ready.

📧 **Calle del Almendro 13**
☎ **91 365 42 52** 🕔 **Lunch, dinner** 🚇 **La Latina**

El Anciano Rey de los Vinos (€)

Founded in 1909, this bar near the Palacio Real is atmospheric, with mirrors and tiles. Try sugary, crunchy *torrijas*, the surprising speciality that is a perfect partner for their own sweet muscatel wines.

📧 **Calle de Bailén 19** ☎ **91 532 14 73** 🕔 **Lunch, dinner. Closed Sun, Aug** 🚇 **La Latina**

Antigua Casa Angel Sierra (€)

Traditional and decorated in old-Madrid style. This 1917 vermouth bar has painted glass and rows of bottles. Vermouth with (*con sifón*) or without soda, is served from a massive brass tap, as is beer. Simple *tapas* are made in front of you.

📧 **Calle de la Gravina 11**
☎ **91 531 01 26** 🕔 **Lunch, dinner** 🚇 **Chueca**

Café Figueroa (€)

In the heart of Barrio de Chueca, the gay district, this is the best known of the gay bars. Unremarkable during the day, crowded after 9PM.

📧 **corner of Calle de Hortaleza and Augusto Figueroa**
☎ **91 521 16 73** 🕔 **Lunch, dinner** 🚇 **Gran Vía**

Los Caracoles (€)

Handy for the Rastro Flea Market, and therefore especially busy on Sundays, the house speciality is snails, but there are plenty of other *tapas* available, all washed down with cheap red wine or beer.

📧 **Plaza de Cascorro 18**
☎ **91 365 94 39** 🕔 **Lunch, dinner. Closed Sun dinner** 🚇 **La Latina**

Casa Alberto (€)

Legend has it that Cervantes came here while writing *Don Quixote*. Order a *Vermut de Grifo* (draught vermouth drawn from a splendid antique pump) and try the *albóndigas* (meatballs).

📧 **Calle de Las Huertas 18**
☎ **91 429 93 56** 🕔 **Lunch, dinner. Closed Sun dinner, Mon** 🚇 **Sol, Tirso de Molina**

Casa Labra (€)

The birthplace of the PSOE (Spanish Socialist Party) in 1879, this *taberna* reeks of tradition. The speciality is *soldaditos de Pavía*, mouthfuls of deep-fried cod. Off Puerta del Sol.

📧 **Calle de Tetuán 12**
☎ **91 531 00 81** 🕔 **Lunch, dinner. Closed Sun, public hols** 🚇 **Sol**

Casa Paco (€)

You can't get more typical than this old-fashioned, city-centre tavern. The classic, simple *tapas* are based on high-quality *jamón* Serrano and Manchego cheese. A handy spot south of the Plaza Mayor.

✉ **Plaza de la Puerta Cerrada 11** ☎ **91 366 31 66** ◷ **Lunch, dinner. Closed Sun, Aug**
Ⓜ **La Latina, Sol**

Los Gabrieles (€)
No point in looking for a sign; listen for the noise and you'll find it. Century-old hand-painted wall tiles depict scenes from *Don Quixote*.

✉ **Calle de Echegaray 17** ☎ **91 429 6261** ◷ **Mon–Thu 12:30PM–2AM, Fri, Sat 12:30PM–3AM** Ⓜ **Sevilla, Sol**

Lhardy (€€)
Best known as a luxury restaurant (▶ 94). The bar looks like a grocery store but sells everything from hot soup to a delicate *fino* sherry from a silver urn. Near Puerta del Sol.

✉ **Carrera de San Jerónimo 8** ☎ **91 521 33 85** ◷ **Lunch, dinner. Closed Sun, public hols dinner** Ⓜ **Sol, Sevilla**

Museo Chicote (▶ 54)

Stop Madrid (€)
On a street full of restaurants and bars, this stands out for its array of colourful wall tiles. But the wine, beer and *tapas* are the main attraction.

✉ **Calle de Hortaleza 11** ☎ **91 531 52 84** ◷ **Lunch, dinner** Ⓜ **Gran Via**

Taberna de Antonio Sánchez (€)
Named in honour of the bullfighter Antonio Sánchez, and founded by his father. *Aficionados* meet below the bull's head mounted on the wall of the oldest tavern (1830) in Madrid.

✉ **Calle Mesón de Paredes 13** ☎ **91 539 78 26** ◷ **Lunch, dinner. Closed Sun dinner** Ⓜ **Tirso de Molina**

Taberna de Cien Vinos (€)
This 'tavern of 100 wines' in one of the oldest parts of town has a lively young clientele. Join them to sample a wide range of Spanish wines.

✉ **Calle del Nuncio 17** ☎ **91 365 47 04** ◷ **Lunch, dinner. Closed Mon** Ⓜ **La Latina**

La Trucha (€)
Just off the Plaza Santa Ana, this is a sister of the nearby restaurant. Regulars stand at the bar, drinking chilled red house wine by the glass and sampling a wide array of *tapas*. Choose fish, meat or vegetables grilled *a la plancha*.

✉ **Calle Manuel Fernández y González 3** ☎ **91 429 58 33** ◷ **Lunch, dinner** Ⓜ **Antón Martín, Sevilla**

La Venencia (€)
If a chair is propping the door ajar, this 1929 bar is open for business. Sample sherries, from the sweetest to the driest. Simple *tapas*, *mojama* (salty dried tuna) and olives.

✉ **Calle de Echegaray 7** ☎ **91 429 73 13** ◷ **Lunch, dinner. Closed Aug** Ⓜ **Sevilla, Sol**

La Venta de Don Jaime (€)
In a basement in the Argüelles district, this is a simple, authentic Andalucian bar, with tiles, barrels of sherry and Andalucian *tapas* such as *chanquetes* (fried whitebait).

✉ **Calle de Alberto Aguilera 36** ☎ **91 445 49 03** ◷ **Lunch, dinner. Closed Sun dinner, 2 weeks in Aug** Ⓜ **Argüelles**

Viva Madrid (€)
You can't miss this bar, with its tiled picture of Cybeles outside. The clientele is young and lively. Just off Plaza de Santa Ana.

✉ **Calle Manuel Fernández y González 7** ☎ **91 429 36 40** ◷ **Lunch, dinner** Ⓜ **Sevilla**

Tapas
There are hundreds of combinations of *tapas*. Here are a few of the most common.
albóndigas: meatballs
callos: tripe
croquetas: potato croquettes
gambas: prawns
jamón: dried ham
mojama: dried tuna
morcilla: black pudding
pescaito, *boquerones*, *chanquetes*: fried fish
pimientos rellenos: stuffed red peppers
tortilla: potato omelette

Cafés and Bars with a Difference

Coffee

Drinking coffee is a way of life in Madrid. A small, black espresso is a *café solo*, a weaker, American-style coffee is an *americano*, while black with just a splash of milk is a *cortado* ('cut' with milk). Milky coffee, which is usually only taken with breakfast, is *café con leche*. Decaffeinated coffee is more readily available than it used to be: ask for *descafeinado*. In summer a *café con hielo* (iced black coffee) is surprisingly refreshing.

El Balcón de Rosales (€)

On the pretty *paseo* overlooking the Casa de Campo, this disco-bar is popular with the younger set who come here for Tex-Mex food. Even the Spanish love karaoke.

✉ **Paseo del Pintor Rosales**
☎ **91 541 74 40** 🕐 **8PM–dawn. Closed Mon–Wed**
Ⓜ **Argüelles**

Bar-Cafetería San Miguel (€)

In the middle of the San Miguel Market, this is where traders do deals and celebrate with a coffee and an *anis*, a small glass of aniseed-flavoured liqueur from Chinchón.

✉ **Plaza de San Miguel**
☎ **91 541 24 09** 🕐 **7–2, 4–8. Closed Sun** Ⓜ **Sol**

Bruin (€)

One of Madrid's favourite places for home-made ice-cream, with 32 flavours including sherry and orange with Cointreau. Buy a cone or sit at a table outside; simple seating upstairs.

✉ **Paseo del Pintor Rosales 48**
☎ **91 541 59 21** 🕐 **12PM–8PM; Jul–Sep 10AM–2AM**
Ⓜ **Argüelles**

Café de los Artistas (€)

Find this café underground, beneath the Plaza Colón, near the entrance to the Centro Cultura de la Villa de Madrid. Serves lunch, then *tapas* and sandwiches until 10PM.

✉ **Jardines del Descubrimiento, Plaza Colón**
☎ **91 431 85 10** 🕐 **Lunch, snacks in evening** Ⓜ **Colón**

Café de los Austrias (€)

Portraits of royals and marble tables help to recreate the Madrid of 100 years ago.

This busy and popular café is big and bright and overlooks the square.

✉ **Plaza de Ramales 1**
☎ **91 559 84 36** 🕐 **9AM–1AM. Closed Mon PM** Ⓜ **Opera**

Café de Oriente (€)

It doesn't matter what time your tour of the Palacio Real finishes, this elegant café will be open, serving *tapas*, sandwiches, pizzas and *pâtisseries*. Sit outdoors in summer.

✉ **Plaza de Oriente 2** ☎ **91 541 39 74** 🕐 **8:30AM–1:30AM, weekends to 2:30AM** Ⓜ **Opera**

Café Viena (€)

Madrid's answer to a Viennese coffee house – ornate décor with gilt and red velvet. Live piano music every evening during dinner. On Monday, light operetta is a speciality.

✉ **Calle de Luisa Fernanda 23**
☎ **91 559 46 45** 🕐 **Lunch, dinner. Closed Sun**
Ⓜ **Ventura Rodríguez**

Cafetería Serrano (€)

Next to Marks & Spencer on the Calle del Serrano, this is popular with shoppers. Sit outside, at the bar, or in a booth upstairs; order coffee and light meals.

✉ **Calle del Serrano 50**
☎ **91 435 77 07** 🕐 **Lunch, dinner** Ⓜ **Serrano**

Cervecería Alemana (€)

Yet another watering-hole where Hemingway once drank, this 1904 German-style beer house even uses steins. Wood panelling and white marble-topped tables add to the atmosphere.

✉ **Plaza de Santa Ana 6**
☎ **91 429 70 33**
🕐 **11AM–12:30AM, Fri, Sat to**

2AM. Closed Tue, Aug

🚇 Antón Martín, Sevilla, Sol

Cervecería Bocata y Olé (€)
One of four wildly tiled, modern bars serving *bocatas* (sandwiches) and large salads, this is ideal for a snack in comfort after seeing the Museo Sorolla (► 20).

✉ General Martínez Campos 2
☎ 91 445 72 83 🕐 9AM–1AM. Closed Sun 🚇 Iglesia

Chocolatería San Ginés (€)
All green tiles and mirrors, this small café is a favourite for hot chocolate and *churros*. At 3:30AM it is packed with partygoers from the nightclub next door.

✉ Pasadizo de San Ginés 5
☎ 91 365 65 46 🕐 7PM–7AM
🚇 Sol

El Despertar (€)
With live jazz on Friday and Saturday, this small café in the Lavapies district is popular with students.

✉ Torrecilla del Leal 18
☎ 91 530 80 95 🕐 7PM–2AM
🚇 Anton Martín

Embassy (€)
Founded in 1931, this sophisticated boulevard café-tea room has its own *pâtisserie*, specialising in mouth-watering, French-style cakes. It also serves cocktails and elegant snacks. Branches at Ayala 3 and La Moraleja.

✉ Paseo de la Castellana 12
☎ 91 435 94 80 🕐 9:30AM–1AM 🚇 Colón, Serrano

El Espejo (€)
Espejo means 'mirror', and the tall, elegant mirrors are just part of the appeal of this art nouveau café on the stylish part of the *paseo*. Choose one of the outdoor tables and enjoy people-watching.

✉ Paseo de Recoletos 31 ☎ 91 308 23 47 🕐 10:30AM–1AM
🚇 Banco de España, Colón

Gran Café Gijon (€)
Open since 1888 and still one of Madrid's most popular meeting places, particularly for those in the film and theatre industry. A well-priced *menu del día* as well as snacks.

✉ Paseo de Recoletos 21
☎ 91 521 54 25 🕐 8 AM–1:30AM
🚇 Banco de España, Colón

Naturbier (€)
There are several bars selling beer on this teeming square, but this one brews its own German-style beer, best accompanied by German sausages. Expect tourists and students. Sit outside when it's fine.

✉ Plaza de Santa Ana 9
☎ 91 249 39 18 🕐 11:30AM–2AM, Fri, Sat to 3AM
🚇 Antón Martín, Sol

Net Café (€)
Madrid has several cyber-cafés where visitors can drink coffee and check their e-mail. This one is in the heart of town, and has eight computers.

✉ Calle de San Bernardo 81
☎ 91 594 09 99 🕐 10AM–2AM
🚇 San Bernardo

Populart (€)
Late-night live music is the speciality at this 'Café Jazz'. Expect to pay a small cover charge to listen to jazz plus anything from flamenco to reggae.

✉ Calle de las Huertas 22
☎ 91 429 84 07 🕐 4PM–2:30AM 🚇 Antón Martín

La Sastrería (€)
Opened in 1997, with a theme of hangers and mirrors, the name means 'the tailor's shop'. A stylish spot for quality coffee during the day; gay clientele in the evening.

✉ Calle de Hortaleza 74
☎ 91 532 07 71
🕐 10AM–2AM 🚇 Chueca

Cheers!
In most bars, inexpensive red wine is the norm, served in a *chato*, which is about the size of a shot glass. However, Madrid has a number of bars that specialise in *vermút*, slightly bitter but refreshing draught vermouth drawn from a barrel, either straight or *con sifón* (with soda water). Bars that have an Andalucian flavour specialise in sherry, and you can choose anything from dry *finos* to sweet *olorosos*.

Outside Madrid

Spanish Regional Dishes

Madrid is an international city, with the cuisines of the world represented, but there are also restaurants and cafés serving food from all regions of Spain. The Valencian style of cooking means rice-based dishes, especially *paella*. In Asturias, *sidra* (cider) is used in cooking and is also drunk with the meals. Both Galicia and the Basque country are well known for the excellence of their fish and shellfish. Catalan cooking tends to be innovative and Mediterranean. Always ask for the regional wine that goes with these regional dishes.

Alcalá de la Henares
Hostería del Estudiante (€€)

In one of the 15th-century student colleges, now carefully restored and open as a restaurant serving Castilian dishes.

✉ **Calle de los Colegios 3**
☎ **91 888 03 30**
🕐 **Lunch, dinner. Closed Aug**

Aranjuez
Casa José (€)

To eat asparagus and strawberries where they are grown there's nowhere better than this high-class restaurant, regarded as the best in town.

✉ **Calle de los Abastos 32**
☎ **91 891 14 88** 🕐 **Lunch, dinner. Closed Sun dinner, Mon**

Chinchón
Parador Nacional de Turismo (€–€€)

Just off the Plaza Mayor, this converted former convent and cloisters is a delightful oasis of calm and elegance. Fine restaurant, local dishes.

✉ **Calle Generalísimo 1**
☎ **91 894 08 36**
🕐 **Lunch, dinner**

El Escorial
Parilla Príncipe (€–€€)

A restaurant set in an 18th-century palace. Fish dishes make a welcome change from the typical mountain fare of so many restaurants.

✉ **Calle de Floridablanca 6**
☎ **91 890 16 11**
🕐 **Lunch, dinner**

La Granja de San Ildefonso
Restaurante Zaca (€)

Eating here is like eating in a Spanish home, with hearty dishes such as ox tongue and stews. Family-run for 60 years. Worth booking.

✉ **Calle de los Embajadores 6**
☎ **92 147 00 87** 🕐 **Lunch only**

Manzanares el Real
Taurina (€–€€)

A useful spot to eat in the middle of this historic town. Best to order local dishes and local wines.

✉ **Plaza Generalísimo 8**
☎ **91 853 07 73** 🕐 **Lunch, dinner. Closed Tue, Aug**

El Pardo
La Marquesita (€€)

Game and roast meats are the specialities of this old restaurant near the Pardo Palace.

✉ **Avenida de la Guardia 29**
☎ **91 376 03 77**
🕐 **Lunch, dinner**

Segovia
La Floresta (€€)

Eat roast suckling pig in one of the small dining rooms or in the courtyard among a fountain and flowers.

✉ **Calle de San Agustín 27**
☎ **921 46 33 14**
🕐 **Lunch, dinner**

Toledo
La Abadía (€–€€)

Next to the Iglesia de San Nicolás, this informal restaurant is in the brick cellar of a 16th-century mansion. Above-average cooking, and unusual *tapas*.

✉ **Plaza San Nicolás 3** ☎ **925 25 07 46** 🕐 **Lunch, dinner**

Casón de los López de Toledo (€€)

Lamb with figs is among the enterprising dishes served in this converted mansion. Courtyard with plants downstairs; upstairs is the elegant dining-room.

✉ **Calle de la Sillería 3** ☎ **925 25 47 74** 🕐 **Lunch, dinner**

Madrid

Apartohotel Eraso (€)
This 3-star hotel in the Salamanca district, is good value for families and has 31 modern rooms. Own garage.

⊠ **Calle de Ardemans 13**
☎ **91 355 32 00, fax 91 355 66 52; www.aphotel-eraso.com**
Ⓠ **Diego de León**

Hotel Alcalá (€€–€€€)
This 146-room hotel has surprisingly stylish rooms with lots of polished wood. Helpful staff.

⊠ **Calle de Alcalá 66** ☎ **91 435 10 60, fax 91 435 11 05; www.nh-hoteles.es**
Ⓠ **Príncipe de Vergara**

Hotel Asturias (€)
Over 100 years old, this 170-room hotel was renovated recently. Good for bargain accommodation in the middle of the city.

⊠ **Calle de Sevilla 2** ☎ **91 429 66 76, fax 91 429 40 36; www.chh.es** Ⓠ **Sevilla**

Hotel Emperador (€€)
With 241 rooms right in the middle of town, this is popular with package tour organisers, but the rooms are spacious and there is the bonus of a roof-top pool.

⊠ **Gran Vía 53** ☎ **91 547 28 00, fax 91 547 28 17; www.emperadorhotel.com**
Ⓠ **Gran Vía**

Hotel Lagasca (€€)
A 3-star hotel near the shops of the Serrano and surrounded by good restaurants. Opened in the early 1990s, its 100 rooms are plain, in minimalist style; striking bathrooms.

⊠ **Calle de Lagasca 64**
☎ **91 575 46 06, fax 91 575 16 94; www.nh-hoteles.com**
Ⓠ **Velázquez**

Hotel Moderno (€€)
This 3-star hotel is only moments from the Plaza Mayor and the Puerta del Sol. Families welcome.

⊠ **Calle del Arenal 2**
☎ **91 531 09 00, fax 91 531 35 40; www.hotelmoderno.com**
Ⓠ **Sol**

Hotel Moncloa Garden (€€)
A modern 3-star hotel, popular with business people during the week and overseas holidaymakers at weekends. Handy for the Metro, with a hearty breakfast buffet.

⊠ **Calle Serrano Jover 1**
☎ **91 542 45 82, fax 91 542 71 69; www. hotelmoncloagarden.com**
Ⓠ **Argüelles, Ventura Rodriguez**

Hotel Mora (€)
Recently redecorated budget hotel with 62 rooms, just across from the Prado (► 26).

⊠ **Paseo del Prado 32** ☎ **91 420 05 64, fax 91 429 15 69**
Ⓠ **Atocha**

Hotel Opera (€–€€)
A smart, contemporary 3-star hotel handy for the Teatro Real, the Palacio Real (► 23) and the old quarter. Public parking near by.

⊠ **Cuesta de Santo Domingo 2**
☎ **91 541 28 00, fax 91 541 69 23; www.hotelopera.com**
Ⓠ **Opera**

Hotel Orense (€€)
Just off the Paseo de la Castillana and near the Real Madrid football stadium, this 140-room, 4-star hotel is also ideal for the business district.

⊠ **Calle de Pedro Teixeira 5**
☎ **91 597 15 68, fax 91 597 12 95; www.hotelorense.com**
Ⓠ **Estadio Bernabéu**

Prices
Prices are based on the cost of a double room per night. Rates rarely include breakfast or tax.
€ = under €100
€€ = €100–150
€€€ = over €150
Although most hotels have air-conditioning, it is worth double-checking that your room will be cool during the summer months. If the hotel is on a main street, ask for a room at the back.

Money-saving Tip
If you are going to Madrid for a weekend, you can often get a reduced rate. Another money-saving system is run by Bancotel, who have 300 participating hotels in Spain. Buy a Bancotel chequebook with five cheques and you can save up to 65 percent on the usual rates. For details, ☎ 906 321 322 (Spain), +34 915 096 109 (international), www.bancotel.com, or call your local travel agent. They also offer reductions on car hire and golf.

Hotel Palace (€€€)
Built in 1913, this Westin 5-star hotel lives up to its name, from the stained-glass dome over the huge lobby to the gymnasium, garage, two restaurants and 144 rooms. A short walk from Madrid's three famous art museums.
✉ **Plaza de las Cortes 7**
☎ **91 360 80 00, fax 91 360 81 00; www.palacemadrid.com**
🚇 **Banco de España**

Hotel París (€)
A centrally-located, 121-room hotel overlooking the Puerta del Sol; attractive prices. More a place to lay your head than to spend time relaxing, though the interior *patio* is an oasis. Ask for an air-conditioned room.
✉ **Calle de Alcalá 2** ☎ **91 521 64 96, fax 91 531 01 88**
🚇 **Sol**

Hotel Ritz, Madrid (€€€)
Dating from 1910, this was the first grand, international hotel in Madrid. Five stars, 156 rooms, three restaurants, one in the flower-filled garden, and a fitness centre. A luxurious, if expensive experience, near museums and Retiro Park (➤ 24).
✉ **Plaza de la Lealtad 5**
☎ **91 701 67 67, fax 91 701 67 76; www.lemeridien-ritzmadrid.com**
🚇 **Banco de España**

Hotel Santo Mauro (€€€)
Models and pop stars check in to this former palace for peace and style. All 36 rooms are individually decorated, with modern furnishings. Marble fireplaces and an old library hark back to the 19th century.
✉ **Calle de Zurbano 36**
☎ **91 319 69 00, fax 91 308 54 77; www.ac-hoteles.com**
🚇 **Rubén Darío**

Hotel Serrano (€€)
Completely refurbished in 1999, this 4-star hotel is now an intimate retreat in the heart of the Salamanca district. Some rooms accessible for people with disabilities; own bar, garage.
✉ **Calle del Marqués de Villamejor 8** ☎ **91 435 52 00, fax 91 435 48 49; www.hotelserranoroyal.com**
🚇 **Serrano**

Hotel Suecia (€€)
Practical rather than pretty, the Suecia has 128 modern rooms and a seventh floor terrace for sunbathing.
✉ **Calle del Marqués de Casa Riera 4** ☎ **91 531 69 00, fax 91 521 71 41; www.hotelsuecia.com**
🚇 **Banco de España**

Hotel Tryp Monte Real (€€–€€€)
On the northwest edge of Madrid, near the Puerta de Hierro golf course and the motorway. With 80 luxury rooms, this quiet 5-star hotel is ideal for business meetings. The Real Madrid footballers stay here before big matches.
✉ **Calle del Aroyo Fresno 17**
☎ **91 316 21 40, fax 91 316 39 34; www.solmelia.com**

Hotel Tryp Reina Victoria (€€€)
You can't miss the ornate tower of this 4-star hotel, with 201 rooms, where bullfighters traditionally stay. Overlooks the bars and cafés of the Plaza de Santa Ana.
✉ **Plaza de Santa Ana 14**
☎ **91 531 45 00, fax 91 522 03 07; www.solmelia.com** 🚇 **Sol**

Hotel Villa Magna (€€€)
Stars of the film and pop world stay here in 5-star luxury, near the main business district and upmarket Calle del Serrano shopping. There are 182 rooms, two restaurants, plus 350-space car park.
✉ **Paseo de la Castellana 22**
☎ **91 587 12 34, fax 91 575 31 58; www.madrid.hyatt.com**
🚇 **Colón**

Outside Madrid

Chinchón
Parador Nacional de Turismo (€€–€€€)
Get away from it all in this converted 15th-century convent. Wander in the gardens, with their pear trees and jasmine, or swim the pool. Elegant restaurant (► 83).

✉ **Calle Generalisimo 1**
☎ **91 894 08 36, fax 91 894 09 08; www.parador.es**

El Escorial
Hotel Victoria Palace (€€–€€€)
A grand 4-star hotel with 90 rooms, just 200m from the famous monastery-palace. Swimming pool, restaurants.

✉ **Calle de Juan de Toledo 4**
☎ **91 890 15 11, fax 91 890 12 48;**
www.hotelvictoriapalace.com

Parilla Príncipe (€)
A restaurant with rooms (► 100) in an 18th-century palace. The 23 bedrooms are simple but comfortable.

✉ **Calle de Floridablanca 6**
☎ **91 890 16 11; www.inicia.es**

Segovia
Ayala Berganza (€€)
A 15th-century palace converted into a stylish, modern 4-star hotel. The look is minimalist, with the ancient walls and arches adding character. Luxurious bedrooms, private parking.

✉ **Calle de Carretas 5** ☎ **92 146 04 48, fax 92 146 23 77; www.partner-hotels.com**

Hotel Infanta Isabel (€)
Converted into a hotel in 1992, this 19th-century building overlooks the Plaza Mayor. Ask for a room with a balcony so that you can admire the cathedral. Good breakfast but no restaurant.

✉ **Plaza Mayor** ☎ **92 146 13 00, fax 92 146 22 17;**
www.infantaisabel.com

Parador de Segovia (€€)
113-room hotel surrounded by trees and lawns, only 3km from Segovia's famous aqueduct. Restaurant, gymnasium, sauna and two swimming pools.

✉ **Carretera de Valladolid**
☎ **92 144 37 37, fax 92 143 73 62; www.parador.es**

Toledo
La Almazara (€)
Excellent city views from this well-priced hotel that was once an archbishop's summer home, and was supposedly visited by the artist El Greco. Private parking.

✉ **Carretera de Toledo, Cuerva (3.4km from city)** ☎ **92 522 38 66, fax 92 525 05 62; www. ribernet.es/hotel_almazara**

Hostal del Cardenal (€)
What was once the home of the powerful archbishops of Toledo has been converted into a 27-room hotel. Eighteenth-century touches remain, as does the lovely garden. The restaurant is highly rated.

✉ **Paseo de Recaredo 24**
☎ **92 522 49 00, fax 92 522 29 91; www.cardenal.asernet.es**

Parador del Conde de Orgaz (€€)
The best feature of this modern hillside hotel is its sunset views of the city across the river. The 148 bedrooms are plain, but comfortable. The restaurant serves local specialities.

✉ **Paseo de los Cigarrales**
☎ **92 522 18 50, fax 92 522 51 66; www.parador.es**

The Paradores of Spain
Spain has long been famous for its *paradores*, a government-run chain of hotels. These are often converted castles and monasteries in attractive locations with reasonably priced rooms. They make a point of serving regional dishes in their restaurants. Central reservations

☎ **91 516 66 66, fax 91 516 66 57;**
www.parador.es

Clothes, Jewellery & Accessories

Department Stores

Spain's most popular department store group is El Corte Inglés. As well as fashion, fabrics and accessories, they sell everything from toiletries to camera film and batteries. With well-priced restaurants, they are usually open from 10–9, and do not close for lunch. Central branches include:

Calle de Preciados 3
Plaza de Callao 2
Calle de Goya 76 and 87
Calle de Raimundo
 Fernandez Villaverde 79
Calle de la Princesa 42
Calle de Serrano 47

Fashion for Men and Women

Adolfo Domínguez

Although the top international designers are represented in Madrid, Spain has its own superstars. Adolfo Domínguez has seven fashion and accessory shops, including several in the Serrano shopping area.

✉ **Calle de Serrano 18**
☎ **91 577 82 80** 🚇 **Serrano**

Agatha Ruiz de la Prada

When you are looking for something out of the ordinary, whether for men or women, this store could be just the place. Just off the Paseo de la Castellana.

✉ **Calle del Marqués del Riscal 8** ☎ **91 310 44 83**
🚇 **Rubén Darío**

Cortefiel Hombre and Cortefiel Mujer

One of the most popular chains, selling men's and women's clothing. There are eight branches in Madrid selling everything from designer fashions to reasonably priced, everyday wear.

✉ **Calle de Serrano 40**
☎ **91 431 33 42** 🚇 **Serrano**

Guadarnés

Modern classics with a casual look: these clothes are in natural fabrics just right for hot climates. In the ABC Serrano shopping centre, store 108 is for women, 128 is for men. Another branch is at the Arturo Soria Plaza shopping centre.

✉ **Calle de Serrano 61**
☎ **91 578 39 19**

Jésus del Pozo

Near the Plaza de Cibeles and off the Paseo de Recoletos, this shop features one of Spain's leading and most famous young designers.

✉ **Calle del Almirante 9**
☎ **91 531 36 46** 🚇 **Colón**

Mango

At last count, there were nine branches of this highly successful chain, selling stylish clothes in stylish settings. Mainly for the young and young-at-heart, who recognise good value when they see it.

✉ **Calle de Goya 83**
☎ **91 435 39 58** 🚇 **Goya**

Roberto Verino

This Spanish designer has several stores in central Madrid, with clothes and accessories for men and women.

✉ **Calle de Claudio Coello 27**
☎ **91 577 73 81** 🚇 **Serrano**

Varade

Spain is known for its fine leathers, so Madrid is the place to buy gloves. A wide range of styles, colours and finishes are available in this specialist shop in the heart of the fashion district.

✉ **Calle de Serrano 54**
☎ **91 575 67 41** 🚇 **Serrano**

Yanko

Yanko's elegant shoes are well known all across Spain and sold in major department stores. Their flagship store displays their latest men's and women's designs.

✉ **Calle de Lagasca 52**
☎ **91 576 16 78** 🚇 **Serrano**

Zara

Up-to-the-minute styles at low prices have made this chain of stores a success not just in Spain but internationally as well. This is one of five branches in Madrid.

✉ **Gran Vía 32**
☎ **91 522 97 27** Ⓜ **Gran Vía**

Fans and Capes

Almoraima
It may look like a shop just for tourist souvenirs, but ask about *abanicos* and you will be shown fans made of everything from plastic to ivory and ebony, factory-made and hand-painted.

✉ **Plaza Mayor 12**
☎ **91 365 42 89** Ⓜ **Sol**

Casa de Diego
Most women in Madrid still carry a fan in their handbag for hot weather or as a fashion accessory. This old-fashioned fan and umbrella shop sells a huge range; the best are works of art, costing as much as a painting.

✉ **Puerta del Sol 12**
☎ **91 522 66 43** Ⓜ **Sol**

Seseña
The cape is both Spanish and romantic. For about 100 years, Seseña has been famous for its ready-made and tailor-made capes for men and women.

✉ **Calle de la Cruz 23**
☎ **91 531 68 40** Ⓜ **Sol**

Jewellery

Ansorena
In business for over 150 years and jewellers to the royal family in that time, Ansorena is synonymous with fine jewellery in Madrid. Everything from ropes of pearls to diamond-studded tiaras are on display at their glamorous store.

✉ **Calle de Alcalá 52 and 54**
☎ **91 532 85 15**
Ⓜ **Banco de España**

Leather Goods

Camper
Madrid is full of shoe shops, but this is one of the most popular, part of a country-wide chain. Well-priced, good styles for men and women, including some that are fun and just that little bit different.

✉ **Calle de Ayala 13**
☎ **91 431 43 45** Ⓜ **Serrano**

Gala
If you need another suitcase to carry home your extra purchases, then Gala is the place for a wide range of luggage as well as fine leather handbags, made by Spanish and also international manufacturers.

✉ **Centro Commercial ABC Serrano, Serrano 61**
☎ **91 578 23 06** Ⓜ **Serrano**

Loewe
Enrique Loewe started a leather goods shop in Calle Echegaray back in 1846. Since then the company has won the title of Proveedora de la Real Casa (By Royal Appointment) and is still a world-famous leader for quality.

✉ **Calle de Serrano 26 and 34**
☎ **91 577 60 56** Ⓜ **Gran Vía**

Manuel Herrero
Near Puerta del Sol, there are two branches of this leather goods shop on the same street (at No 16 and No 7). Good for shoes and jackets in suede and special skins.

✉ **Calle de Preciados 16**
☎ **91 521 15 24** Ⓜ **Sol**

Zapatería Albaladejo
A step inside and you breathe in the wonderful smell of fine leather that pervades this shoe shop. You can buy ready-made or be measured for a pair of handmade shoes. A Mallorcan business since 1890, this shop opened here in 1997.

✉ **Calle de Claudio Coello 73** ☎ **91 576 40 90**
Ⓜ **Serrano**

Shopping Areas
The best-known, and most expensive, shopping area of Madrid is on and around the Calle de Serrano (► 34). Other good hunting grounds include the Gran Vía, and the area around Puerta del Sol, especially Calle de Preciados. Near the University, on the northwest side of the city, Calle de la Princesa has young, trendy shops. Around Chueca, new boutiques and galleries are opening every day.

Arts, Crafts, Gifts & Design

Palacios y Museos
This is the place to buy reproductions of famous pieces from the world's most famous museums. Typically Spanish gifts include decanters based on designs from the 18th-century glass factory at La Granja, gold cufflinks based on pre-Colombian artefacts, and fans made of polished pear wood.

✉ Arturo Soria 126
☎ 91 338 72 65

El Angel
Spain is known for its shops selling religious items, ranging from pictures of saints and nativity scenes to nuns' habits. El Angel is one of the best.

✉ Calle de Esparteros 3
☎ 91 532 04 91 🚇 Sol

Antigua Casa Crespo
This old-fashioned shop is known for selling *alpargatas*, espadrilles, or rope-soled shoes, that come in all shapes and sizes. You can also buy leather sandals here.

✉ Calle del Divino Pastor 29
☎ 91 521 56 54
🚇 San Bernardo, Bilbao

El Arco de los Cuchilleros
In the heart of the tourist district, this building houses 30 or more craftsmen and women, producing contemporary jewellery, textiles and ceramics. Well priced and well worth a look.

✉ Plaza Mayor 9
☎ 91 365 26 80 🚇 Sol

El Bazar de Doña Pila
Bazar is the right word for this shop, which is stacked high with arts and crafts from Spain and all over the world: glass, *papier mâché*, ceramics and carved wood.

✉ Calle del Divino Pastor 31
☎ 91 522 59 19
🚇 San Bernardo

B D Ediciones de Diseño
Although this shop is best known for showcasing the finest of Spanish and international furniture designers, they also sell smaller items such as trays, pitchers and chic kitchenware.

✉ Calle de Villanueva 5
☎ 91 435 06 27
🚇 Serrano, Retiro

Cántaro
Spanish pottery and ceramics always make good souvenirs and presents. This shop near the Gran Vía has a wide range, representing every corner of Spain. The only difficulty is making a choice!

✉ Calle de la Flor Baja 8
☎ 91 547 95 14 🚇 Santo Domingo, Plaza de España

La Casa de los Chales
Spanish shawls, with their characteristic embroidery and fringe, come in all sorts of fabrics and a multitude of designs. Prices are just as broad ranging. Here, you can choose from wool as well as velvet and lace.

✉ Calle de Maiquez 3
☎ 91 409 72 39 🚇 Goya

Casa Jiménez
Spanish *mantillas* may not be a practical gift for visitors from foreign countries, but *mantonas* (shawls) can make useful and attractive presents. The shawls in this well-known specialist shop are often described as works of art. Find it just off the Gran Vía.

✉ Calle de Preciados 42
☎ 91 548 05 26 🚇 Callao

Futbol Total
A couple of former footballers have set up a shop selling an extraordinary range of football shirts from all over Spain and the world. Pick your shirt, have your name and number printed on it right there, and you're a member of your favourite team.

✉ Calle de Eloy Gonzalo 7
☎ 91 593 35 99
🚇 Iglesia, Quevedo

Jose Cerrón
Baskets are a traditional part of Spanish life and this is a

good place to buy one.
Among the wide variety of
shapes and styles, you can
find baskets for eggs and for
your cat!

✉ **Calle de Augustín Durán 16**
☎ **91 726 02 23**
🚇 **Diego de León**

Lola Fonseca
Lola Fonseca was a stock-
broker before changing
career and using her talent
for painting on fabric. Now
she decorates everything
from shawls and silk scarves
to ties and cushions.

✉ **Calle de Santa Isabel 50**
☎ **91 530 65 22** 🚇 **Atocha**

López
The silversmiths of Spain
have been famed through
the centuries. This firm
has worked for the royal
court and offers high-quality
craftsmanship and a wide
range of merchandise –
from a silver ink stand to
a baby rattle.

✉ **Calle del Prado 3** ☎ **91
429 63 71** 🚇 **Banco de España**

La Mansión del Fumador
Everything for the smoker,
from pipes to ash trays and
from lighters to cigar cutters.
Surprisingly, they do not
sell tobacco.

✉ **Calle del Carmen 22**
☎ **91 532 08 17** 🚇 **Sol**

María José Fermín
This traditional wrought-iron
worker is on the street that
becomes the Rastro Flea
Market (▶ panel) on
Sunday. In addition to
barbecues, chairs and
tables, he makes attractive
weather vanes adorned with
cockerels and witches.

✉ **Ribera de Curtidores 9**
☎ **91 539 43 67** 🚇 **La Latina**

Martínez
Alpargatas (espadrilles or
rope-soled shoes) may be
the traditional footwear of
the Spanish peasant, but
they are also ideal for the
beach. This shop is in the
Salamanca district, near the
Calle de Serrano.

✉ **Calle de Claudio Coello 72**
☎ **91 431 14 16** 🚇 **Serrano**

Museo Nacional Centro de Arte Reina Sofía
The excellent shop has the
widest range of modern art
books in the city, as well as
cheap mementoes such
as *Guernica* key rings and
pencil cases.

✉ **Calle Santa Isabel 52**
☎ **91 467 50 62** 🚇 **Atocha**

Museo Thyssen-Bornemisza
Down in the gift shop of this
museum is a wide choice of
reproductions of the most
famous paintings in the
museum. Best sellers include
Gauguin's hot-coloured South
Pacific scene, *Mata Mua*
(1892); find it on everything
from expensive silk scarves
to simple posters.

✉ **Paseo del Prado 8** ☎ **91
420 39 44** 🚇 **Banco de España**

Pérez A Fernández
It's worth going along to this
century-old silversmiths, just
to look at the exterior of this
beautiful shop. Inside, the
handcrafted silver is based on
traditional Galician designs.

✉ **Calle de Zaragoza 3**
☎ **91 366 42 79** 🚇 **Opera**

Quetzal
A wide range of crafts
imported from India and
Nepal, plus others from
South and Central America.

✉ **Calle Mayor 13**
☎ **91 364 25 76** 🚇 **Sol**

Rastro Flea Market
The Sunday morning El
Rastro is legendary (▶ 65).
Many stalls sell modern
handicrafts, such as model
planes and boats made
from recycled soft drink
cans, scented candles,
wood carvings and leather
belts and handbags. This is
a good place to shop for
inexpensive souvenirs
and gifts.

Antiques, Books & Music

Read All About It!
Wander along Calle de Claudio Moyano, on the south side of the Real Jardín Botánico (➤ 70), to have a look at the stalls of the Mercado del Libro. This open-air, second-hand book market is busiest on Sunday mornings, but some stalls are open during the week. At the end of May and beginning of June, *La Feria del Libro* (Madrid's book fair), attracts crowds to Parque del Retiro, where hundreds of stalls representing publishers and bookshops are set up.

Antigüedades Siglo 20
The name means '20th-century antiques', and Juan Ramón Salazar has three shops in the Galerías Piquer antique market. His speciality is furniture and art deco objects, including mirrors, clocks and even three-piece suites.
- ✉ **Calle de Ribera de Curtidores 29** ☎ **91 530 45 40**
- 🚇 **La Latina**

La Casa del Libro
The largest bookstore in Spain, with five floors in a classic art nouveau building. As well as thousands of Spanish titles, there is a useful corner selling books and guides in several foreign languages.
- ✉ **Gran Vía 29**
- ☎ **91 521 21 13** 🚇 **Gran Vía**

Casa Postal
The postcards we send today are the collectors' items of tomorrow. This old-fashioned shop is a rummagers delight, crammed with old and antique postcards, as well as maps, photographs and 'curiosities', such as train sets and unused calendars from 1949. Any special requests are ably handled by Martín Carrasco Marqués, the proud owner.
- ✉ **Calle de la Libertad 37**
- ☎ **91 532 70 37** 🚇 **Chueca**

Félix Manzanero
What could be more Spanish than the guitar? Manzanero served an apprenticeship with the legendary José Ramírez and now has his own shop, where both professionals and amateurs come to buy handcrafted instruments. He also has on display antique guitars, dating back to the 18th century.
- ✉ **Calle de Santa Ana 12**
- ☎ **91 366 00 47**
- 🚇 **La Latina, Tirso de Molina**

El Flamenco Vive
The de la Plaza family claim that this is the only shop dedicated to the art of flamenco or what they call the Spanish 'blues'. They sell everything from guitars to memorabilia. Buy some shoes, a video and an instruction book and you're ready to learn to dance.
- ✉ **Calle de Conde de Lemos 7**
- ☎ **91 547 39 17** 🚇 **Opera**

Galerías Piquer
Most of the score of antique shops that overlook the quiet courtyard have old-fashioned, rather heavy Spanish antiques. Go during the week to avoid the crowds on a Sunday.
- ✉ **Calle de Ribera de Curtidores 29** 🚇 **La Latina, Puerta de Toledo**

International Bookshop
A useful shop for foreign visitors, this is a treasure trove of mostly second-hand books in every category you can think of and in half a dozen different languages.
- ✉ **Calle de Campomanes 13**
- ☎ **91 541 72 91**
- 🚇 **Santo Domingo**

Mercedes Cabeza de Vaca
On the street that hosts the Sunday Rastro Flea Market (➤ 65), Mercedes specialises in late 19th- to early 20th-century porcelain dolls, although she also sells table lamps, mirrors and clocks.
- ✉ **Calle de Ribera de Curtidores 12** ☎ **91 530 64 43**
- 🚇 **La Latina**

Food & Drink

Casa Mira
Turrón (nougat) is the national confectionery of Spain, and comes in a wide variety of flavours. This shop is owned by the descendants of a *turrón*-maker from Alicante, who brought his special recipe to Madrid in the 19th century. The mixture of almonds and honey is still made by hand.
- ✉ Carrera de San Jerónimo 30
- ☎ 91 429 88 95 🚇 Sevilla

Churrería Moral
Next door to the Casa Museo Lope de Vega (► 35), this tiny, family-run shop makes fresh *patatas fritas* (crisps) and *churros*.
- ✉ Calle de Cervantes 9
- ☎ 91 429 48 38
- 🚇 Antón Martín

Felipe Sánchez
This is a really old-fashioned shop, specialising in a wide range of sweets (toffees, bonbons, biscuits) and dried fruits and nuts (almonds, hazelnuts, walnuts, peanuts).
- ✉ Plaza San Andrés 4
- ☎ 91 365 36 34 🕐 Mon–Fri 9–2, 5–8, Sat 9–2 🚇 La Latina

Horno San Onofre
Come here to sample the regional variety of Spanish cakes and tarts, as well as seasonal ones, traditionally made to celebrate saints' feast days. The speciality is the sponge cake-like *tarta de Santiago*.
- ✉ Calle de San Onofre 2
- ☎ 91 532 90 60 🚇 Gran Vía

Licores Cabello
This one-customer-at-a time shop is a former *bodega* (wine cellar) down a side street. Despite its tiny size, it stocks over 500 table wines, regional liqueurs and dusty bottles of Rioja dating back to the 1920s.
- ✉ Calle de Cervantes 6
- ☎ 91 429 52 30
- 🚇 Antón Martín

La Mallorquina
This cake shop, which has a second branch, has been a feature of the Puerta del Sol since 1894. Locals come to buy biscuits and buns, chocolates, sweets and cakes for a special occasion.
- ✉ Puerta del Sol 8/ Calle Mayor 2 ☎ 91 521 12 01
- 🕐 Mon–Sat 10–3, 5–8
- 🚇 Sol

Museo del Jamón
This restaurant-shop is one of a chain that are hung with haunches of ham. The choice is enormous.
- ✉ Calle de Alcalá 155
- ☎ 91 431 72 96 🚇 Atocha

El Palacio de los Quesos
The Palace of Cheeses has all the Spanish specialities. Manchego, for example, is available *tierno* (young) to *añejo* (mature). They even have the strong-tasting *curado*, matured in oil. Try *cabrales*, a blue-veined, full-flavoured mixture of goat and sheeps' milk cheese from Asturias.
- ✉ Calle Mayor 53 ☎ 91 548 16 23 🚇 Sol, Opera

Patrimonio Comunal Olivarero
In a country where olive oil is used in virtually every dish, it is not surprising to find a shop that sells nothing but *aceite de oliva virgen extra*, the best olive oil you can get.
- ✉ Calle de Mejía Lequerica 1
- ☎ 91 308 05 05
- 🚇 Alonso Martínez, Tribunal

What to Take Home
For a wide selection of local delicacies such as *jamón* (ham), sausages and cheese, head for the food halls at El Corte Inglés. Extra virgin olive oils are good buys. You can pick up Spanish wines and vacuum-packed food-stuffs at Barajas Airport.

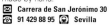

Children's Attractions

Look Behind You!
The ancient art of puppetry is alive and well in Madrid. Take the children to the Parque del Retiro (► 24) on Sunday morning to see knockabout shows that produce howls of laughter and plenty of audience participation. Even if you don't speak Spanish, the language of puppetry is international. Find them by the *estanque* (lake).

As a city Madrid has a limited number of attractions that appeal to the non-Spanish-speaking child. All children, however, are welcome in cafés and restaurants, and local youngsters tend to stay up later than their contemporaries from northern Europe or America.

Acuarium
Right in the middle of the city, this is an unusual combination of pet shop and museum. As well as a diverting display of fish in the *acuario* (aquarium), there are also plenty of creepy-crawlies and reptiles.

✉ **Calle del Maestro Victoria 8** ☎ **91 531 81 72** 🕓 **Daily 11–2, 5–9** 🚇 **Sol, Callao**

Aquamadrid
At San Fernando de Henares, 15km east of Madrid and open since 1987, this is a huge lake in the middle of a wooded park. The rides range from easy (Foam) to the most scary (Kamikaze), which is an 85m-long slide with a 40m drop.

✉ **Carretera Nacional II, 15.5km** ☎ **91 673 10 13** 🕓 **Jun–Sep 12–8** 🚇 **Expensive**

Aquasur
Opened in 1998 and an instant hit, this park is 40km south of the city, near Aranjuez. The most daring water slide is the Espíritubo, a steep, scary tube ride, but there are also gentler water slides for the less adventurous, a zoo, mini-golf and a huge swimming pool.

✉ **Carretera de Andalusía (N–IV) km 44** ☎ **91 891 60 34** 🕓 **Jun–Sep 10:30–8, 11 at weekends** 🚫 **None** 🚇 **Moderate**

Aquópolis
Opened in 1987, Aquópolis claims to be the biggest aquatic park in Europe, with 17 different attractions, including the 40m-high Kamikaze and the popular Tobogán Blando, with a series of harmless jumps and turns. Upgraded in 1999, the park now has more trees and prettier gardens. Find it at Villanueva de la Cañada, about 40km northwest of the city via M 503, exit 8.

✉ **Avenida de la Dehesa, Villanueva de la Cañada** ☎ **91 815 69 11** 🕓 **Jun–Sep 12–8; 11 at weekends** 🚇 **Expensive**

IMAX Madrid
This cinema has three of the universally-popular giant format screens: IMAX, Omnimax and IMAX 3D. Films (mainly wildlife) are changed regularly, usually last about 45 minutes and run throughout the day, seven days a week. Order tickets by phone ahead of time from the central booking number: Servicaixa 902 33 22 22.

✉ **Parque Tierno Galván** ☎ **91 467 48 00** 🕓 **Daily** 🚇 **Méndez Alvaro** 🚇 **Moderate–expensive**

Museo de Cera de Madrid
Madrid's waxwork museum features a mixed bag of famous characters, both historical and contemporary, although the emphasis is definitely Spanish.

✉ **Paseo de Recoletos 41** ☎ **91 319 26 49** 🕓 **Mon–Fri 10–2:30, 4:30–8:30, Sat–Sun 10–8:30** 🚇 **Colón** 🚇 **Moderate**

Parque de Atracciones
This permanent fun-fair in the Casa de Campo (➤ 12) has about 40 rides as well as the usual amusements. One of the latest thrill rides is the Virtual Simulator, which has been added to others with stomach-churning names such as *Los Rápidos* (The Rapids), *Los Fiordos* (The Fjords) with a 15m drop and *La Máquina* (The Machine). The auditorium hosts live music concerts in the summer.

✉ **Casa de Campo** ☎ **91 463 29 00** 🕐 **11–11, Sat 12–1AM. Closed Mon** 🚇 **Batán** 🎫 **Moderate**

Parque del Retiro
There is plenty of room here for children to play and work off energy, but the park is especially fun on a Sunday morning when there are puppet shows on the promenade by the lake (➤ 24).

Real Madrid
One of the world's most famous football clubs has a popular club shop, where their trademark white shirts are a best seller (➤ 44).

✉ **Paseo de la Castellana 144** ☎ **91 457 06 79** 🚇 **Santiago Bernabéu**

Safari de Madrid
Some 40km west of the city, this is a traditional safari park with elephants, giraffes, lions and tigers. There are also reptile and snake houses and, in July and August, a playground with go-karts, mini-motorbikes and a swimming-pool.

✉ **Aldea de Fresno, Carretera de Extremadura, N-V, 32km**

☎ **91 862 23 14** 🕐 **10:30–sunset** 🎫 **Expensive**

Teleférico
Children love this cable-car ride (➤ 71).

Tren de la Fresa
Taking the 'Strawberry Train' down to Aranjuez (➤ 82) is a fun day out for all ages. The old steam train departs from Atocha Railway Station. On the journey, hostesses in period costume hand out some of the strawberries for which Aranjuez is famous. Once in the town, there is plenty of time to enjoy the gardens, riverboat rides and the royal palace

☎ **90 222 88 22** 🕐 **Apr–Oct, excluding Aug** 🎫 **Expensive**

Zoo Aquarium
Another reason to head for the Caso de Campo park, this zoo has over 2,000 animals, including snakes and tigers, plus sharks in the aquarium and a dolphinarium with two shows a day (three in summer). Their mascot is Chu-lin, the giant panda, but the zoo prides itself on having other rare species, such as red pandas and white tigers. The new aviary has been an instant hit, with 60 birds of prey flying free. Recently re-landscaped, the park now looks more attractive. Small children enjoy the little train and also boat rides on the canal, which give a different view of the animals and provide a rest for tired feet! There are plenty of places around here to eat.

✉ **Casa de Campo** ☎ **91 512 37 80** 🕐 **10:30–dusk** 🚇 **Batán** 🎫 **Expensive**

Messing About in Boats
Another amusement in the Parque del Retiro is boating on the *estanque* (lake), under the watchful eye of Alfonso XII. Across the city in the Casa de Campo (➤ 12) is another boating lake.

Bars, Clubs &
Live Music

Late Night Extra
Traffic jams at 2AM are nothing unusual during the summer in Madrid. Thousands spend the early hours chatting and drinking in *terrazas*, which spill across the pavements of the *paseos*, especially the Paseo de la Castellana.

Café Central
Arguably Madrid's best-known jazz café, set in a former grocery shop. The elegant decoration includes a carved wood ceiling and pictures made of leaded, coloured glass. The programme includes artists from the USA as well as Europe.
✉ **Plaza del Angel 10** ☎ **91 369 41 43** 🕐 **2:30PM–2:30AM; weekends to 3:30AM** 🚇 **Sol**

Café de Chinitas
Flamenco originated in the south of Spain, but is popular in the capital. Enthusiastic audiences are mainly Spanish, though foreigners are also fans. This restaurant, set in the basement of a 17th-century palace, has nightly shows starting at 10:30PM.
✉ **Calle de Torija 7** ☎ **91 559 51 35** 🕐 **9PM–dawn. Closed Sun** 🚇 **Santo Domingo**

Café Habana
Cuban culture is trendy nowadays and this club serves cocktails and hot Cuban music. Order a *mojito* (a potent drink of rum, lime and mint).
✉ **Calle de las Infantas 30** ☎ **91 532 44 57** 🕐 **1PM–dawn** 🚇 **Chueca**

Chesterfield Café
Opened in 1997, the theme here, like the name, is American, with American bands and American beer.
✉ **Calle de Serrano Jover 5** ☎ **91 542 28 17** 🕐 **12–3:30AM. Closed Mon** 🚇 **Argüelles**

Big Bamboo
Ideal for a rowdy night out, with pounding reggae music, vigorous dancing and bizarre cocktail rituals, such as drinking a margarita upside down.
✉ **Calle de Barquillo 42** ☎ **91 562 88 38** 🕐 **10PM–dawn** 🚇 **Alonso Martínez**

Clamores
Although the speciality is jazz, you can expect almost any act to turn up here, including reggae, blues and Latin American folk. Shows start at 10:30PM.
✉ **Calle de Alburquerque 14** ☎ **91 445 79 38** 🕐 **7PM–3AM** 🚇 **Bilbao**

Fortuny
If your idea of fun is to brush shoulders with the stars, the Fortuny is one of the celebrity sanctuaries of Madrid, where Bruce Willis, Brad Pitt and others are supposed to hide from their fans. However, there is a very strict dress code at this glitzy nightclub in a converted mansion.
✉ **Calle de Fortuny 34** ☎ **91 319 05 88** 🕐 **2PM–dawn** 🚇 **Rubén Darío**

Garamond
In the heart of the most fashionable district of Madrid, this is one of the most fashionable discos. The main difficulty is getting through the door; dress smartly, look affluent and you may be ushered through to see how the other half dances.
✉ **Calle de Claudio Coello 10** ☎ **91 578 19 74** 🕐 **6PM–dawn** 🚇 **Retiro**

Houdini Club de Magia
The Spanish still enjoy a good, old-fashioned magician. This club also has a rather spooky atmosphere.
✉ **Calle de Fuencarral 21**

COVER CHARGE

☎ 91 521 06 70 🕔 9PM–3AM
🚇 Gran Vía

Joy Madrid
The lovely old Teatro Eslava (1872) has seen it all, from the old music hall shows to variety sketches. Now the three tiers of seating encircle Madrid's hottest nightclub.
✉ Calle de Arenal 11
☎ 91 366 54 39 🕔 11PM–5AM
🚇 Sol

Moby Dick
Hugely popular, hot and sweaty, this club has a varied programme of live music and DJs throughout the week.
✉ Avenida de Brasil 5 ☎ 91 555 72 81 🕔 10PM–5AM. Closed Sun 🚇 Lima

No Se Lo Digas a Nadie
The cheeky name, meaning 'don't tell anyone about it', was invented by the women's co-op that runs this relaxed disco in the middle of town. Downstairs is disco dancing; upstairs are half a dozen pool tables.
✉ Calle de Ventura de la Vega 7 🕔 9PM–3AM. Closed Sun 🚇 Sevilla

Noches de Cuplé
A nostalgic night out for the older generation of Spanish, but thoroughly enjoyed by the younger one as well. This is traditional Spanish music hall entertainment with a floorshow by Olga Ramos and her daughter Olga Maria.
✉ Calle de la Palma 51
☎ 91 532 71 15 🕔 9PM–3AM
🚇 San Bernardo

Palacio de Gaviria
This is not a made-up name. The handsome 19th-century mansion plays host to a variety of music in a dozen surprisingly elegant rooms. Dress code is smart, prices are justifiably high.
✉ Calle de Arenal 9
☎ 91 526 60 69 🕔 11PM–5AM
🚇 Sol

La Riviera
If you are young and love big, live rock concerts, then this is definitely the best place to go in the city.
✉ Paseo Virgen del Puerto
☎ 91 365 24 15 🕔 Check listings 🚇 Puerto del Angel

La Tolderia
This club specialises in Latin-American folk music, attracting big names from South America. Popular with ex-patriates as well as the Spanish.
✉ Calle de los Caños Viejos 3
☎ 91 366 41 72 🕔 11PM–dawn. Closed Sun, Mon
🚇 La Latina

Tropical House
The theme of this disco is salsa and tango. Tuesday is tango only; Sunday is devoted to Latin-American ballroom dancing.
✉ Calle de Martín de los Heros 14 ☎ 91 541 59 37
🕔 11PM–dawn
🚇 Plaza de España

Villa Rosa
With its tiles on the outside and Moorish design inside, you could guess that this disco was once a flamenco club. There are still flamenco nights as well as salsa nights, but most of the time it's a busy disco.
✉ Plaza de Santa Ana 15
☎ 91 521 36 89
🕔 11PM–dawn. Closed Sun
🚇 Sol

Gay Madrid
Madrid has the second biggest gay community in Europe, centred on the Chueca district, just north of the Gran Vía. In the small squares and narrow streets are bars, shops, discotheques and some of the best new restaurants in the city. The atmosphere is relaxed, with gays, lesbians and the straight community mixing (🚇 Chueca).

Theatre, Cinema, Music & Dance

What's Up?

When it comes to entertainment, Madrid has several weekly guides to what is on in the city. Free, pocket-sized bi-lingual magazines such as the tourist board's *En Madrid qué hacer* (*What's On in Madrid*) and *Lo Mejor de Madrid* (*The Best of Madrid*) give the highlights for international visitors. By far the most comprehensive listings are in the 180-page *Guía del Ocio* (*Leisure Guide*), which has every event, major and minor, but this is only in Spanish.

Casa de América

This cultural centre dedicated to things Latin American (➤ 34) has daily presentations of film, plays and music that are worth checking out.

✉ **Paseo de Recoletos 2**
☎ **91 595 48 00** 🎟 **Box office: 9–2, 4–6. Closed Sat, Sun** 🚇 **Banco de España**

Centro Cultural Conde Duque

Although this cultural centre (➤ 38) has a busy programme year round, it is at its best in the summer (mid-June to mid-September) when the courtyard is taken over by the Veranos de la Villa, a summer festival of jazz, classical music, ballet and opera. Several other sites in the city also take part in this festival.

✉ **Calle de Conde Duque 11**
☎ **91 588 58 34** 🎟 **Box office: 10:30–2, 5:30–9. Closed Mon** 🚇 **Ventura Rodríguez, Noviciado, San Bernardo**

Centro Cultural de la Villa

This modern cultural centre is situated underground, behind the waterfall of the Plaza Colón. As the city's official cultural centre, it stages a wide variety of performances year round, but is particularly known for *zarzuela* (light opera) and dance.

✉ **Plaza de Colón** ☎ **91 575 60 80** 🎟 **Box office: 11–1:30, 5–8. Closed Mon** 🚇 **Colón**

Círculo de las Bellas Artes

This arts complex has a small but attractive theatre, as well as a library and café.

✉ **Calle del Marqués de Casa Riera 2** ☎ **91 532 44 37**
🚇 **Banco de España**

Teatro Monumental

This auditorium is the home of the orchestra of Spain's national television station. The season runs from October to April. In addition to the well-priced concerts, there are performances of *zarzuela* and opera.

✉ **Calle de Atocha 65**
☎ **91 429 81 19**
🎟 **Box office: 11–2, 5–7**
🚇 **Atón Martín**

Teatro Real

The 1990s saw this theatre restored to its 1850s grandeur and it has now joined the ranks of Europe's great opera houses. The season runs from September to July, and since opera is very popular, tickets can be difficult to come by. There are regular backstage tours (Tuesday–Friday at 10:30, 11:30 and 12:30).

✉ **Plaza de Oriente** ☎ **91 516 06 60** 🎟 **Box office 10–1:30, 5:30–8. Closed Sun. Tickets also from the Caja de Madrid: 902 488 488** 🚇 **Opera**

Teatro de la Zarzuela

Zarzuela is the light opera of Spain and Madrid is considered its home. Spanish light opera may not get the recognition that serious opera receives, but it is worth noting that Plácido Domingo, whose parents were *zarzuela* singers, has recorded popular songs in this style. The theatre was built in 1856 and is a copy of La Scala in Milan.

✉ **Calle de Jovellanos 4**
☎ **91 524 54 00** 🎟 **Box office 12–6. Closed Mon. Tickets also from the Caja de Madrid: 902 488 488**
🚇 **Banco de España**

Sport

Spectator Sports

Basketball

Real Madrid's basketball team has a record that is almost as dazzling as the football squad. Along with fellow first division Estudiantes, Real play in the Palacio de Deportes de Madrid from September to May.

⊠ **Avenida de Felipe II**
☎ **91 401 91 00** ⏰ **Box office: 11–2, 5–8** Ⓜ **Goya**

Football

For Real Madrid details (▶ 44, 111).
Perennial rivals of Real Madrid, Atlético Madrid play in a huge 60,000-seat stadium. Their ambitious chairman is constantly changing managers and bringing in new star players in an attempt to recapture the form of 1996 when they won the league and cup.

⊠ **Estadio Vicente Calderón**
☎ **91 366 47 07** ⏰ **Box office: 5–8. Closed Sat, Sun** Ⓜ **Pirámides**

Participatory Sports

Golf

With the success of Seve Ballesteros and José María Olazábal, golf is enjoying a boom in Spain. Although it can be an expensive past-time, there is a good choice of 18-hole golf courses around Madrid.

Club de Campo Villa de Madrid
⊠ **Carretera de Castilla, 2km**
☎ **91 550 08 40** Ⓟ **84**

Club Valdelaguila
⊠ **Carretera Villabilla, 8km**
☎ **91 885 96 59**

La Dehesa
⊠ **Avenida Universidad, Villanueva de la Cañada**
☎ **91 815 70 22**

Real Club Puerta de Hierro
⊠ **Avenida Miraflores**
☎ **91 316 17 45**

La Moraleja
⊠ **Paseo Marquesa Viuda de Aldama 50, La Moraleja**
☎ **91 650 07 00**

Ice-skating

This sport is still relatively novel in a nation that prefers to skate on wheels, but you can hire ice-skates and helmets at the indoor Sport Hielo.

⊠ **Estación de Chamartín**
☎ **91 315 63 08** ⏰ **9–1, 5–9, Sat, Sun 9–9. Closed Jul, Aug** Ⓜ **Chamartín**

Skiing

Skiing is popular and on weekends skiers head for the mountains north of the city, an hour or so away by car. Resorts include:
Navacerrada ☎ **91 852 1435, La Pinilla** ☎ **92 155 03 04, Valcotos** ☎ **91 563 30 61**

Swimming

There are several open-air pools run by the city. In the Casa de Campo, there are three, one for children, one intermediate and one of Olympic size. All are busy on summer weekends. See also Aquamadrid, Aquasur and Aquópolis (▶ 110).

⊠ **Casa de Campo, Avenida del Angel** ☎ **91 463 00 50**
⏰ **May–Sep 10:30–8**
Ⓜ **Largo**

Bullfighting

Opinions differ on the role of bullfighting. Is it a sport, an art form or an integral part of Spain's national identity? The decision is very individual. In recent years, *corridas* (fights) have drawn ever-more enthusiastic crowds to the Plaza de Toros of Las Ventas, the world's most famous arena, in the east of the city (▶ 63).

What's On When

San Isidro
Although the feast day of San Isidro, Madrid's patron saint, is on 15 May, the festival lasts for three weeks. After mass on 15 May, a pilgrimage crosses the Río Manzanares, and locals in traditional dress drink water from a fountain (which has been blessed), picnic on *rosquillas* (sweet buns) and dance. Theatre, concerts and 28 bullfights, rated the world's most prestigious, are all part of the festivities.

January
Cabalgata de los Reyes Magos (5 Jan): the evening procession of the Three Kings leads on to the next day's *Epifanía* (Epiphany), when the kings throw sweets to children lining the streets.

February
ARCO (Feb): Contemporary Art Fair, a leading event for top artists, dealers and collectors from all over the world, although it is less successful now than it has been in the past.
Carnaval: before Lent, Madrid parties. A ceremony called the *Entierro de la Sardina* (the Burial of the Sardine), takes place in the Casa del Campo (► 12).

March/April
Semana Santa (Holy Week): celebrated with solemn processions of penitents through the streets.

May
Dos de Mayo (2 May): Madrid remembers the day when *madrileños* rose up against the French in 1808.
Festimad (early May): once an 'alternative' festival but now big business right across the spectrum – films, poetry readings, music, dance and more in the Bellas Artes building and in Móstoles, in the suburbs.
San Isidro (15 May): Madrid's patron saint.
Feria del Libro (the Festival of the Book): held in the Parque del Retiro where booksellers set up hundreds of stalls (► 24).

June
San Antonio de la Florida (13 Jun): At the Ermita de San Antonio de la Florida, unmarried girls visit the chapel to make them lucky in love (► 39).
San Juan (17–24 Jun): fireworks in the Parque del Retiro to celebrate the festival of St John (► 24).
Los Veranos de la Villa (Jun–Sep): a season of music, theatre, *zarzuela*, dance and open-air cinema, put on under the auspices of the Villa de Madrid; the main venue is the Conde-Duque cultural centre.

July
Virgen del Carmen (16 Jul): local festivals for the Virgin in the suburbs of Chamberí, Villaverde and Vallecas.

August
San Cayetano, San Lorenzo (10 Aug), the *Virgen de la Paloma* (15 Aug): local *fiestas* in La Latina, Argumosa and Lavapiés.

October/November
Festival de Otoño: a festival involving all the performing arts based round a theme, for example a country or literary figure.

November
Fiesta de la Almudena (9 Nov): festival of the (female) patron saint of Madrid.

December
Feria de Artesanía (Dec–6 Jan): Advent craft fair centred on the Paseo de Recoletos (► 59).
Nochevieja (New Year's Eve): thousands of people fill the Puerta del Sol to watch the clock and follow the tradition of swallowing one grape at each of the 12 strokes of midnight.

Practical Matters

Above: *Metro entrance,*
Puerta del Sol
Right: *it's good*
to talk

117

TIME DIFFERENCES

GMT	Madrid	Germany	USA (NY)	Netherlands	France
12 noon	1PM →	1PM →	← 7AM	1PM →	1PM →

BEFORE YOU GO

WHAT YOU NEED

● Required ○ Suggested ▲ Not required	Some countries require a passport to remain valid for a minimum period (usually at least six months) beyond the date of entry – contact their consulate or embassy or your travel agent for details.	UK	Germany	USA	Netherlands
Passport		●	●	●	●
Visa		▲	▲	▲	▲
Onward or Return Ticket		▲	▲	●	▲
Health Inoculations		▲	▲	▲	▲
Health Documentation (► 123, Health)		●	●	●	●
Travel Insurance		○	○	○	○
Driving Licence (national with Spanish translation or International)		●	●	●	●
Car Insurance Certificate (if own car)		●	●	●	●
Car Registration Document (if own car)		●	●	●	●

WHEN TO GO

Madrid

High season

Low season

9°C	11°C	15°C	18°C	21°C	27°C	31°C	30°C	25°C	19°C	13°C	9°C
JAN	FEB	MAR	APR	MAY	JUN	JUL	AUG	SEP	OCT	NOV	DEC

 Very wet   Wet   Cloud   Sun   Sun/showers

TOURIST OFFICES

In the UK
Spanish Tourist Office
22/23 Manchester Square
London
W1U 3PX
☎ 020 7486 8077
Fax: 020 7486 8034
www.tourspain.es

In the USA
Tourist Office of Spain
666 Fifth Avenue
(35th Floor)
New York
NY 10103
☎ (212) 265 8822
Fax: (212) 265 8864

Tourist Office of Spain
8383 Wilshire Boulevard
Suite 960
Beverley Hills
CA 90211
☎ (213) 658 7192
Fax: (213) 658 1061

EMERGENCY 112

POLICE 091 (National), 092 (Madrid)

FIRE 080

AMBULANCE 061, RED CROSS 91 522 22 22

WHEN YOU ARE THERE

ARRIVING

Aeropuerto de Barajas, east of the city, has three terminals: T-1 for international flights; T-2 for national and as well as some Iberia flights within Europe, and T-3 for regional flights and the Madrid-Barcelona shuttle. General enquiries ☎ 91 393 60 00. Flight information ☎ 91 305 83 43. In 1999 a metro link with the city was opened. Madrid is served by the world's major airlines.

Aeropuerto de Barajas kilometres to city centre	Journey times	
15 kilometres	🚇	30 minutes
	🚌	45 minutes
	🚗	25 minutes

MONEY

Since 1 January 2002, the peseta has given way to the euro, which is divided into 100 cents (or *centesimi*). Coins come in denominations of 1, 2, 5, 10, 20 and 50 cents, 1 and 2 euros, and notes come in 5, 10, 20, 50, 100, 200 and 500 euro denominations (the last two are rarely seen). The notes and one side of the coins are the same throughout the European single currency zone, but each country has a different design on one face of each of the coins. Notes and coins from any of the other countries can be used in Spain.

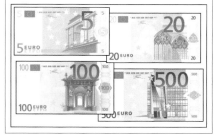

TIME

 Madrid is on CET (Central European Time), one hour ahead of GMT (Greenwich Mean Time). Summer time starts on the last Sunday in March and ends on the last Sunday of October.

CUSTOMS

 YES

From another EU country for personal use (guidelines):
800 cigarettes, 200 cigars,
1 kilogram of tobacco
10 litres of spirits (over 22%)
20 litres of aperitifs
90 litres of wine, of which 60 litres can be sparkling wine
110 litres of beer

From a non-EU country the allowances are:
200 cigarettes OR 50 cigars OR 250 grams of tobacco
1 litre of spirits (over 22%)
2 litres of fortified wine (eg sherry), sparkling wine or other liqueurs
2 litres of still wine
50 ml of perfume
250ml of eau de toilette
Travellers under 17 are not entitled to the tobacco and alcohol allowances.

 NO

Drugs, firearms, ammunition, offensive weapons, obscene material, unlicensed animals.

UK	USA	Germany	Netherlands	France
91 308 52 01	91 587 22 00	91 557 90 00	91 353 75 00	91 700 78

WHEN YOU ARE THERE

TOURIST OFFICES

Tourist and Cultural information Line
☎ 010 (91 366 66 04 outside Madrid)

Oficina Municipal de Turismo
● Plaza Mayor 3
  ☎ 91 366 54 77

Oficinas de Información Turística de la Communidad de Madrid
● Calle Duque de Medinaceli 2
  ☎ 91 429 49 51

Also at
Puerta de Toledo Market
● Stand 3134
  ☎ 91 364 18 76

Estación de Chamartín
● Chamartin Railway Station
  ☎ 91 315 99 76

Barajas Airport
● T-1 Terminal (international arrivals)
  ☎ 91 305 86 56

Madrid Tourist Information website: munimadrid.es

NATIONAL HOLIDAYS

J	F	M	A	M	J	J	A	S	O	N	D
2		1	1	3			1		1	2	3

1 Jan	Año Nuevo (New Year's Day)
6 Jan	Reyes (Three Kings)
Mar/Apr	Jueves Santo, Viernes Santo (Easter Thursday, Good Friday)
1 May	Fiesta del Trabajo (May Day)
2 May	Día de la Comunidad (Madrid Day)
15 May	San Isidro (Madrid's patron saint)
15 Aug	Virgen de la Paloma (Assumption)
12 Oct	Día de la Hispanidad (Discovery of America Day)
1 Nov	Todos los Santos (All Saints' Day)
9 Nov	Virgen de la Almudena
6 Dec	Día de la Constitución (Constitution Day)
8 Dec	La Inmaculada (Immaculate Conception)
25 Dec	Navidad (Christmas)

OPENING HOURS

○ Shops	● Attractions/museums
● Offices	● Restaurants (Lunch)
● Banks	● Pharmacies

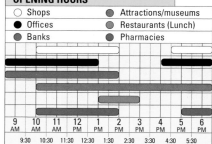

9 AM	10 AM	11 AM	12 PM	1 PM	2 PM	3 PM	4 PM	5 PM	6 PM
9:30	10:30	11:30	12:30	1:30	2:30	3:30	4:30	5:30	

Major museums are open all day, but close on Monday or Tuesday. Smaller museums close for lunch. Shops vary, with most open Monday to Saturday. Some close Saturday afternoon, and most close all day Sunday. Department stores and malls are open 10–9. Many restaurants and shops close during August. During the San Isidro festival in May, banks close at noon. In July and August many offices work straight through from 8 to 3, then close. Apart from opening for mass, well-known churches have set opening hours.

DRIVE ON THE RIGHT

TOILETS FREE

PUBLIC TRANSPORT

Internal Flights
Iberia, the national carrier, has regular flights linking Madrid with other major cities in Spain. The most frequent are between Madrid and Barcelona, with the *Puente Aéreo* (shuttle service) operating from 7AM–11PM.

Trains
The main office of RENFE (Spanish National Railways) is at Calle de Alcalá 44. Tickets and information are also available at Barajas Airport and the three main stations. From Atocha, trains are mainly to southern Spain. The AVE high-speed service to Seville leaves from Puerta de Atocha. From Chamartín, trains go to the north, northeast and France. Travellers can get discounts on some journeys if they travel on so-called 'blue days', marked on calendars available from any RENFE office. A special card for tourists gives unlimited travel on the system.

Buses
Estación Sur de Autobuses, the city's main bus station, is at the corner of Calle Méndez Alvaro and Calle Retama. Near by are the Atocha Railway Station and Méndez Alvaro Metro station. Although buses cover the whole of Madrid, the system is somewhat complicated to understand and it is easier to take the Metro.

Metro
The easiest way to get around Madrid, apart from on foot, is by Metro. The 11-line, colour-coded system has stops close to all the major attractions. The direction of the train is shown by the name of the terminus station. Trains run 6AM–1:30AM. Fares are inexpensive. If you buy a *bono de diez viajes*, (10-ride ticket for Metro or bus), you get a discount.

CAR RENTAL

As usual in large airports, all the major car rental companies are represented at Barajas Airport. They also have offices in the middle of Madrid, but you could choose to rent from a local agency. The minimum age for hiring a car is 21.

TAXIS

Official taxis are white with a diagonal red stripe. Look for the *libre* (free) sign behind the windscreen or a green light on top of the cab. Fares are reasonable. Make sure the meter is not running when you get in. Travel from the airport costs extra.

DRIVING

Speed limit on motorways: **120kph**

Speed limit on main roads: **100kph**

Speed limit on minor roads: **90kph**

Seat belts must be worn in front seats and rear seats where fitted.

Fines are heavy for driving under the influence of alcohol or drugs. It is compulsory to take drink/drug tests when requested by police. Failure to comply is a serious offence.

Regulations It is illegal to drive while wearing headphones or using hand-held mobile phones.

Fines for traffic offences are stringent and payment is required on the spot.

Lead-free petrol (*sin plomo*) is readily available. Other types include *super* (4 star), *normal* (3 star) and *gasoleo* (diesel).

Drivers must carry two warning triangles, spare bulbs and fuses and a spare wheel. The towing of motor vehicles is not permitted, except to move a broken-down car out of traffic or to a safe place. Otherwise, only a breakdown vehicle is allowed to tow a broken-down car.

PERSONAL SAFETY

As in most big cities, pickpockets are a problem in Madrid, especially in busy places such as open-air markets, large shops and railway stations. Valuables such as tickets and passports should be locked up in the hotel rather than carried with you. The Rastro Flea Market is a place where you need to be particularly careful. Madrid is a late-night city, but stay on main streets where there are more people. Be sure to take official taxis only (▶ 121).

City Police
☎ **092**
Emergency
☎ **112**

ELECTRICITY

The power supply in Madrid

is 220 volts AC; sockets have two-pin plugs. If you have a British appliance, you will need an adaptor; North American appliances also require a transformer.

TELEPHONES

There are plenty of telephone booths in the streets. Local calls are inexpensive. Although you can pay with coins, it is quicker and easier to buy a phonecard from any *tabaco* (tobacconist). Many phones also take credit cards. Long-distance calls

are cheaper from a booth than from your hotel. Directory information is 003.

International Dialling Codes
From Madrid to:
UK:	00 44
Germany:	00 49
USA and Canada:	00 1
Netherlands:	00 31
France:	00 33

POST

The main post office, the Palacio de Comunicaciones, is on the Plaza de la Cibeles, open Mon–Sat 8AM–12PM, Sun 8AM–10PM. Elsewhere, *correos* (post offices) are open Mon–Sat 9–2. Stamps (*sellos*) are also sold in any *tabaco*, the tobacconist shop identified by the brown and yellow sign. To post a letter, look for yellow post boxes.

TIPS/GRATUITIES

Yes ✓ No ✗		
Restaurants	✓	5–10%
Cafés/bars (if service not included)	✓	5%
Tour guides	✓	€1
Hairdressers	✓	5%
Taxis	✓	5%
Chambermaids	✓	€1
Porters (per bag)	✓	€1
Theatre/cinema usherettes	✓	€1
Cloakroom attendants	✓	€1
Toilets	✗	no

PHOTOGRAPHY

What to photograph: The narrow streets in old Madrid, grand buildings and the Parque del Retiro. The Cibeles fountain with the post office behind is a classic Madrid scene.
When to photograph: Morning and late afternoon are best since the strong midday sun flattens perspective and washes out colours.
Where to buy film: Branches of VIPs shops and Corte Inglés (department stores) carry a wide range of film and camera batteries.

HEALTH

Doctors
Under EU law, reciprocal medical arrangements allow EU residents carrying a completed E111 form to have free medical treatment and prescribed medicines in Spain. Non-EU citizens are charged private hospital rates, so insurance is essential. English-speaking doctors are available at the Anglo-American Medical Unit ☎ 91 435 18 23.

Dental Services
EU citizens are not covered by the E111 form for the cost of seeing a dentist. All visitors have to pay the full price of a visit and any treatment. Ask at your hotel's reception desk for advice on the nearest dentist.

Sun Advice
Madrid is at a high altitude and has a dry climate and strong sun, so use sunscreen, lip balm and skin moisturiser in spring and autumn as well as in high summer. Hats and sunglasses also give useful protection.

Drugs
Prescription and non-prescription drugs are sold in *farmacias* (chemists), identified by a green cross. In central Madrid, the Farmacia Central ☎ 91 473 06 72 and the Farmacia Lastra ☎ 91 402 43 63 are open 24 hours a day. If you are on medication, carry photocopies of the prescription.

Safe Water
Madrid is famous for the quality of its drinking water and, unlike many other Spanish cities, it does not have the taste of chlorine. Locals are always aware of the need to conserve water. In bathrooms, the hot tap is labelled 'c' for *caliente*, the cold has 'f' for *frío*.

CONCESSIONS

Concessions Many museums offer free admission to the general public, or citizens of the EU on certain days, or during certain hours. It is important to have a passport or national identity card if you are going to claim a concession.
Senior Citizens The over-65s can gain free entry to many museums and galleries.
Students Reductions are available for students in many museums on production of an ISIC (international student identity card).
Under-18s The under-18s can also gain free entry to many museums and galleries.

CLOTHING SIZES

Spain	UK	Rest of Europe	USA	
46	36	46	36	**Suits**
48	38	48	38	
50	40	50	40	
52	42	52	42	
54	44	54	44	
56	46	56	46	
41	7	41	8	**Shoes**
42	7.5	42	9	
43	8.5	43	10	
44	9.5	44	11	
45	10.5	45	12	
46	11	46	13	
37	14.5	37	14.5	**Shirts**
38	15	38	15	
39/40	15.5	39/40	15.5	
41	16	41	16	
42	16.5	42	16.5	
43	17	43	17	
36	8	36	6	**Dresses**
38	10	38	8	
40	12	40	10	
42	14	42	12	
44	16	44	14	
46	18	46	16	
38	4.5	38	6	**Shoes**
38	5	38	6.5	
39	5.5	39	7	
39	6	39	7.5	
40	6.5	40	8	
41	7	41	8.5	

WHEN DEPARTING

- Check the time of your return flight the day before departure. In 1999 Line 8 was extended to the airport, which now has its own Metro station. But, whether getting to the airport by car or Metro, allow extra time if you are travelling during the morning or afternoon rush hours.

LANGUAGE

The Spanish are pleased when foreigners try to speak their language. Don't worry about making mistakes; although they will correct them, it is always with a smile, and a sincere attempt to understand what you are trying to communicate. English is the most commonly taught foreign language; the younger generation usually know a little and often quite a lot. Although pamphlets in foreign languages are available in the larger museums, signs and guided tours in foreign languages are rare.

accommodation	*alojamiento*	room service	*servicio de habitaciones*
hotel	*hotel*		
bed and breakfast	*pensión*	chambermaid	*camarera*
		bath	*baño*
single room	*habitación individual*	shower	*ducha*
		toilet	*servicio*
double room	*habitación doble*	balcony	*balcón*
one person	*una persona*	key	*llave*
one night	*una noche*	quiet room	*habitación tranquila*
reservation	*reserva*		
lift	*ascensor*		

bank	*banco*	travellers' cheque	*cheque de viaje*
exchange office	*cambio*		
post office	*correos*	credit card	*tarjeta de credito*
coin	*moneda*		
banknote	*billete*	exchange rate	*cambio*
cheque	*cheque*	commission charge	*comisión*
change	*cambio*		

café	*cafetería*	starter	*primer plato*
pub/bar	*bar*	main course	*secundo plato*
breakfast	*desayuno*	dessert	*postre*
lunch	*almuerzo*	bill	*cuenta*
dinner	*cena*	beer	*cerveza*
table	*mesa*	wine	*vino*
waiter	*camarero*	water	*agua*
waitress	*camerera*	coffee	*café*

aeroplane	*avión*	single ticket	*billete de ida*
airport	*aeropuerto*	return ticket	*billete de ida y vuelta*
train	*tren*		
bus	*autobús*	non-smoking	*no fumador*
station	*estación*	car	*coche*
boat	*barca*	petrol	*gasolina*
port	*puerto*	bus stop	*parada*
ticket	*billete*	where is…?	*¿donde está…?*

yes	*sí*	excuse me	*por favor*
no	*no*	you're welcome	*de nada*
please	*por favor*	how are you?	*¿ qué tal?*
thank you	*gracias*	do you speak English?	*¿ habla inglés?*
welcome	*bienvenido*		
hello	*hola*	I don't under-stand	*no entiendo*
goodbye	*adios*		
good morning	*buenos días*	how much?	*¿ cuánto es?*
good afternoon	*buenas tardes*	open	*abierto*
goodnight	*buenas noches*	closed	*cerrado*

Acknowledgements

The Automobile Association would like to thank the following photographers, liibraries and museums for their assistance in the preparation of this book

ALLSPORT UK LTD 44b; ANDALUCIA SLIDE LIBRARY 9b, 65, 79, 117b, 122a, 122c; BRIDGEMAN ART LIBRARY The Spinners, or The Fable of Arachne, c.1657 (oil on canvas) by Diego Rodriguez de Silva y Velasquez (1599–1660), Prado, Madrid, Spain/Peter Willi/Bridgeman Art Library 26b; MARY EVANS PICTURE LIBRARY 10b, 11b, 11c; MUSEO DE AMÉRICA (MADRID) 17b, 17c; REX FEATURES 14b; SPECTRUM COLOUR LIBRARY 85b, 86b; WORLD PICTURES 2, 8b, 82b; www.euro.ecb.int 119 (euro notes).

The remaining photographs are held in the Association's own library (AA PHOTOLIBRARY) and were taken by Michelle Chaplow, with the exception of 49, 50b, 51b, 61a, 68/69, 76, 77, 78, 80, 81, 82a, 83a, 83b, 85a, 86a, 87a, 87b, 88a, 88b, 88c, 89a, 89b, 90a which were taken by J Edmanson; 84, 85c, 90b were taken by Philip Enticknap; front cover (a) bear statue, (b) Plaza de Cibeles, (c) cathedral, (d) flamenco dancer, (f) statue, (g) Gran Via, (h) matador, (i) metro sign, bottom, Plaza Mayor, 29, 61a were taken by Max Jourdan; front cover (e) street sign, (j) statue, back cover building and 5a, 6a, 6c, 7a, 7b, 8a, 9a, 10a, 11a, 12a, 13a, 14a, 18b, 20b, 20/21, 21b, 22b, 27a, 27b, 28a, 28/29, 29a, 30, 32a, 33a, 34a, 34b, 36a, 36c, 38a, 39a, 40, 41, 42, 43a, 44a, 46, 47a, 48a, 50a, 51a, 52, 53a, 53b, 54, 55a, 56a, 57a, 57b, 59, 60a, 66, 67, 69a, 69b, 70a, 71a, 72a, 73, 74a, 75a, 91a, 92, 93, 94, 95, 96, 97, 98, 99, 100, 101, 102, 103, 104, 105, 106, 107, 108, 109, 110, 111, 112, 113, 114, 115, 116, 117a were taken by Rick Strange.

Copy editor: Sally MacEachern Page layout: Barfoot Design

Dear Essential Traveller

**Your comments, opinions and recommendations are very
   important to us. So please help us to improve our travel
   guides by taking a few minutes to complete this simple
   questionnaire.**

*You do not need a stamp (unless posted outside the UK). If you do not want to cut this page
   from your guide, then photocopy it or write your answers on a plain sheet of paper.*

Send to: **The Editor, AA World Travel Guides,
FREEPOST SCE 4598, Basingstoke RG21 4GY.**

Your recommendations…

We always encourage readers' recommendations for restaurants, nightlife
or shopping – if your recommendation is used in the next edition of the
guide, we will send you a *FREE* AA *Essential* **Guide** of your choice.
Please state below the establishment name, location and your reasons
for recommending it.

_____

_____

_____

_____

Please send me **AA *Essential*** _____

(*see list of titles inside the front cover*)

About this guide…

Which title did you buy?
   AA *Essential* _____

Where did you buy it? _____

When? ⊡⊡ / ⊻ ⊻

Why did you choose an AA *Essential* Guide? _____

_____

_____

_____

_____

Did this guide meet your expectations?
   Exceeded ☐   Met all ☐   Met most ☐   Fell below ☐
   Please give your reasons _____

_____

_____

_____

continued on next page…

Were there any aspects of this guide that you particularly liked? _____
_____
_____
_____

Is there anything we could have done better? _____
_____
_____
_____
_____

About you...

Name (*Mr/Mrs/Ms*) _____
  Address _____
  _____
  _____ Postcode _____
  Daytime tel nos _____

Which age group are you in?
  Under 25 ☐   25–34 ☐   35–44 ☐   45–54 ☐   55–64 ☐   65+ ☐

How many trips do you make a year?
  Less than one ☐   One ☐   Two ☐   Three or more ☐

Are you an AA member? Yes ☐   No ☐

About your trip...

When did you book? m m / y y   When did you travel? m m / y y
How long did you stay? _____
Was it for business or leisure? _____
Did you buy any other travel guides for your trip?
  If yes, which ones? _____
  _____

Thank you for taking the time to complete this questionnaire. Please send
  it to us as soon as possible, and remember, you do not need a stamp
  (*unless posted outside the UK*).

Happy Holidays!